Redemption in Romans

John C. Brunt

Pacific Press® Publishing Association
Nampa, Idaho
Oshawa, Ontario, Canada
www.pacificpress.com

Cover design by Gerald Lee Monks
Cover design illustration from Lars Justinen
Inside design by Aaron Troia

Unless otherwise noted, all Scripture quotations are from the HOLY BIBLE, NEW INTERNATIONAL VERSION®. Copyright © 1973, 1978, 1984 by International Bible Society. Used by permission of Zondervan Publishing House. All rights reserved.

Scripture texts credited to NRSV are from the New Revised Standard Version of the Bible, copyright © 1989 by the Division of Christian Education of the National Council of the Churches of Christ in the USA. Used by permission. All rights reserved.

Scriptures quoted from KJV are from the King James Version.

The author assumes full responsibility for the accuracy of all facts and quotations as cited in this book.

You can obtain additional copies of this book by calling toll-free 1-800-765-6955 or by visiting www.adventistbookcenter.com.

Library of Congress Cataloging-in-Publication Data:

Brunt, John, 1943-
  Redemption in Romans / John C. Brunt.
     p. cm.
  ISBN 13: 978-0-8163-2387-6 (pbk.)
  ISBN 10: 0-8163-2387-9 (pbk.)
  1. Bible. N.T. Romans—Theology. I. Title.
  BS2665.52.B78 2010
  227'.107—dc22

                                                    2009053241

10 11 12 13 14 • 5 4 3 2 1

Dedication

To our three grandsons, who bring us such joy:

Marcus Leonin Brunt, born June 17, 2003

Akian Christopher MacLeod, born November 2, 2004

Conlan Alexander MacLeod, born December 6, 2007

Table of Contents

CHAPTER 1

Paul and Rome

Many people consider Romans to be a daunting book. It's the longest of Paul's letters and is filled with heavy theology and big words such as *justification, redemption,* and *expiation,* and it speaks of difficult concepts such as God's "wrath." That's enough to scare even the most diligent Bible student. After all, even Peter said that Paul wrote some things that were "hard to understand" (2 Peter 3:16). It's hardly surprising that some people prefer to stick to the simple teachings of the four Gospels and leave books such as Romans to the scholars.

But Romans wasn't written for scholars. It was written for ordinary Christians in the church at Rome in the first century. The Christians who first experienced the book didn't have the privilege of poring over every word and analyzing each theological concept. In fact, they didn't have the privilege of reading the book at all. They simply heard it. You see, when Paul wrote the letter (it isn't really a book, but a letter), he had to send it to Rome with a messenger. And he couldn't tell the messenger, "Stop at Kinko's on the way and make a copy for everyone in the church." No, every copy had to be written by hand. So those who first experienced Romans heard it read out loud to them, probably in a Sabbath morning worship service. That puts quite a different light on how Paul intended this letter to be understood than what we might be tempted to presume.

When we listen to something being read aloud, we can't analyze all the details. Instead, our ears try to help our minds catch the overall meaning and synthesize the basic message. In other words, we try to catch what the forest is all about, not examine every tree. This isn't to say that analysis is bad, but we may tend to overanalyze rather than try to catch the overall message.

Try to imagine that you are a Christian who lives in Rome in the first century. At this point there are no Christian church buildings. Each Sabbath morning you meet other Christians for worship in the home of Priscilla and Aquila. We know that worship services were held in their home because of Paul's greeting to them at the end of this letter: "Greet Priscilla and Aquila, my fellow workers in Christ Jesus. They risked their lives for me. Not only I but all the churches of the Gentiles are grateful to them. Greet also the church that meets at their house" (Romans 16:3–5).

You've never met Paul, but you have heard Priscilla and Aquila talk about him. They met him when they were in Corinth several years earlier, as we read in Acts 18:1–4: "After this, Paul left Athens and went to Corinth. There he met a Jew named Aquila, a native of Pontus, who had recently come from Italy with his wife Priscilla, because Claudius had ordered all the Jews to leave Rome. Paul went to see them, and because he was a tentmaker as they were, he stayed and worked with them. Every Sabbath he reasoned in the synagogue, trying to persuade Jews and Greeks."

You've heard Priscilla and Aquila tell stories of tentmaking with Paul and of listening to his preaching. They've had all kinds of good things to say about his ministry. And so you were excited to hear that next week a messenger is bringing a letter from Paul. You come to this house church on Sabbath morning with wide-open ears and expectancy in your heart. What will this old friend of Priscilla and Aquila have to say to your church at Rome? Why is he writing to you anyway? After all, he's never been here, and usually, when he writes letters to churches, it's to churches he's founded or at least visited.

So you come in to the atrium of Priscilla and Aquila's small villa, and the messenger—probably a woman named Phoebe (see Romans 16:1, 2)—reads you the whole letter in one sitting, in just a little over an hour. What would you take away from the letter?

I suggest that you actually experiment with this. Try to put yourself in that first-century home and listen to the letter. If you have the Bible on CD or tape, listen to Romans. If you don't, take a modern version and read the letter *out loud* so you proximate the oral experience that the first-century believers in Rome would have had. Then take a few moments to jot down the impressions that emerge from your oral hour with Paul's letter to the Romans.

My guess is that a few major themes will stand out. One is that Paul wanted to put Jews and Gentiles in the same boat when it comes to salvation. He wanted the hostility between them to end, and he sought to show that they should all be one in Christ. It would also be hard to avoid the idea that salvation is available to all, whoever they are, if they'll only trust in God through Christ. You would probably also catch the idea that *faith* and *grace* are important terms for Paul. He uses *grace* twenty-four times and *faith* forty times in the letter. And you would notice that he said salvation comes as a gift from God and not from works we do for which we can pat ourselves on the back. Finally, you would surely realize that Paul wanted all Christians to welcome each other and live together in peace without scorning or judging each other or fighting over minor issues.

Did these ideas make your list? What else did you have on it? We'll explore all these issues in subsequent chapters of this book.

Paul's circumstances and plans

Why did Paul write this letter to a church he had never even visited? It all had to do with his plans for the future, and fortunately, he tells us about those plans right in the book itself. Paul wrote the book of Romans at the end of a three-month stay in the city of Corinth during his third missionary journey. We learn this by comparing the book of Acts with Romans. In Acts 19:21, we read that Paul planned to go to Macedonia, Greece, Jerusalem, and then

Rome. In Acts 20:1–3, we find that Paul went to Macedonia, then spent three months in Corinth (a city in Greece), and then headed for Jerusalem by way of Macedonia.

According to Romans 15:25, 26, when Paul wrote the book of Romans, he had just been to Macedonia and was about ready to leave Greece. It seems he wrote from Corinth, or a suburb of Corinth—the seaport Cenchrea, since that was the home of Phoebe, the woman who took the letter to Rome. So the timing and circumstances of Paul's situation when writing Romans fits his third missionary journey as recorded in Acts.

Paul told about his plans in Romans 15. He wanted to visit the church at Rome. Actually, he stated this in Romans 1. There he said, "I long to see you so that I may impart to you some spiritual gift to make you strong—that is, that you and I may be mutually encouraged by each other's faith. I do not want you to be unaware, brothers, that I planned many times to come to you (but have been prevented from doing so until now) in order that I might have a harvest among you, just as I have had among the other Gentiles" (Romans 1:11–13).

Paul fleshed out this desire in Romans 15 when he made it clear that although he wanted to come to Rome and see the believers there, that wasn't his final destination. He hoped to go on to Spain after he visited Rome. He was especially interested in Spain because as far as he knew, the gospel had never reached there, and he wanted to take the gospel to places where it had never been before. He said,

> So from Jerusalem all the way around to Illyricum, I have fully proclaimed the gospel of Christ. It has always been my ambition to preach the gospel where Christ was not known, so that I would not be building on someone else's foundation. Rather, as it is written:
>
> "Those who were not told about him will see,
>   and those who have not heard will understand."

This is why I have often been hindered from coming to you.

But now that there is no more place for me to work in these regions, and since I have been longing for many years to see you, I plan to do so when I go to Spain. I hope to visit you while passing through and to have you assist me on my journey there, after I have enjoyed your company for a while (Romans 15:19–24).

Paul didn't want to have to build on someone else's foundation. He had covered Asia Minor, and now he wanted to take the gospel to Spain. But for such an operation he needed a support base, and Rome was ideal for that. So he decided to go to Spain with a stop in Rome for some time to have the Roman Christians help him prepare for this new and exciting mission.

But, Paul planned to make another stop before going to either Rome or Spain. He would go to Jerusalem first.

Jerusalem? That was hardly on the way from Greece to Rome! In fact, in Greece, Jerusalem and Rome are in opposite directions. Here are the air distances between these cities:

Corinth to Rome	650 miles
Corinth to Jerusalem	800 miles
Jerusalem to Rome	1,450 miles

So if you were traveling by air, going from Corinth to Rome via Jerusalem would take you sixteen hundred miles out of the way. It would be something like flying through Denver on your way from Chicago to Philadelphia! And Paul wasn't traveling by air. He was traveling by foot and on dangerous ships in rough waters. Why then would he go sixteen hundred miles out of his way when he wanted to go to Rome?

The answer is found in a commitment he had made, a commitment that had deep theological and practical significance for him. He tells us about it in Romans 15:25–27: "Now, however, I am on my way to Jerusalem in the service of the saints there. For Macedonia and

Achaia were pleased to make a contribution for the poor among the saints in Jerusalem. They were pleased to do it, and indeed they owe it to them. For if the Gentiles have shared in the Jews' spiritual blessings, they owe it to the Jews to share with them their material blessings."

We'll discuss this in more detail in the next chapter, which is about Jews and Gentiles. Suffice it here to say that Paul had collected money from the Gentile believers to take to the poor Jewish Christians in Jerusalem as a sign of the unity of Jews and Gentiles in Christ. This commitment was so important to Paul that he was willing to take extra months and risk his life to fulfill it.

So Paul made it clear that he was in Greece and that he planned to go to Jerusalem, on to Rome, and then to Spain. But as important as his trip to Jerusalem was to Paul, he had some fears about it. According to Romans 15:31, he worried that his life might be in danger from unbelieving Jews in Jerusalem. He also worried that the Jewish Christians in Jerusalem might not accept the gift he was bringing from the Gentile believers.

Paul's reason for writing

These plans and worries give us an idea of why Paul wanted to write to the Romans. He wanted to prepare the way for his visit there and thus prepare the way for his visit to Spain as well. So he introduced himself to the people in Rome. He did that in several ways. He gave them an overview of the message he preached as an apostle to the Gentiles. He also built on the relationships he had with people whom he knew in Rome. Although he had never been there, in addition to Priscilla and Aquila he had met a number of other people elsewhere who had since moved to Rome. In the first-century world, all roads really did lead to Rome, and it wouldn't have been unusual for many people who had resided elsewhere or at least visited elsewhere to have ended up in Rome.

But Paul wanted more than just to introduce himself to the people at Rome. He was also concerned about some problems within the Roman church that he had heard about. People were arguing about minor issues and relating to each other judgmentally. (We'll explore these problems in chapter 13 of this book, where we'll study Romans 14.) Paul knew that if the church at Rome was going to be a strong support for him in his mission to Spain, it would have to be a unified church. So he tried to bring the church members into unity. In fact, in many ways Paul wrote the whole first part of Romans, which we generally consider heavy theology, to prepare the way for him to address the practical problems, which he does at the end of the letter. The theological message of salvation by grace through faith puts everyone in the same boat and prepares the way for a practical message of unity in Christ and goodwill among all Christians. It was such goodwill that Paul sought to build up in Rome.

Paul also wrote in order to enlist the prayers and possibly also the practical support of the Romans on behalf of his visit to Jerusalem. He wanted them to pray that the unbelieving Jews wouldn't take his life and that the believing Jewish Christians would accept the gift he brought from the Gentiles. He may have known that some of the Christians in Rome still had some influence in faraway Jerusalem and might even put in a good word for him.

So with his mission in mind, Paul was bold enough to write to the Roman Christians even though he had never visited their city.

But things didn't work out as Paul had planned. His worries about the trip to Jerusalem were well founded. The unbelieving Jews did try to take his life by falsely accusing him of taking a Gentile into the area of the temple that was open only to Jews. (See Acts 21:27–40.) They would have killed Paul on the spot had he not been rescued by Roman soldiers stationed at the fortress Antonia, which overlooked the temple area. Paul was arrested, and he spent the next two years of his life imprisoned in Caesarea, on the west coast of Israel, awaiting trial. But he never got to trial there because the civil authorities were hoping for a bribe from his fellow Christians.

After two years, Paul, who was a Roman citizen, appealed to the emperor in Rome. His appeal was granted, and he was sent to Rome as a prisoner. The journey there took another year, which means it was three years before Paul arrived in Rome. Then he spent two more years in Rome under house arrest awaiting trial. Luke's narrative in Acts ends at this point, so we don't know for sure what happened to Paul from this time on. He probably never made it to Spain.

We don't know whether his other worry, that the saints in Jerusalem might not accept the gift he brought, was valid too. Luke tells the story of Paul's trip to Jerusalem and of his arrest there, but he's silent about the gift, which was Paul's whole reason for going to Jerusalem. This is a strange silence given the importance of the gift in Paul's mind.

The history of the church at Rome

One question remains for us to consider in this introductory chapter. Since Paul had never been to Rome, how did the church there get started? The answer is that we don't know. The New Testament is silent. It could be that some of the Jews who were converted on the Day of Pentecost in Jerusalem took the gospel there, but that's only speculation. We simply don't know.

We do know that there were Christians in Rome by about A.D. 49. We know this from both the Bible and secular history. We've already noticed that according to Acts 18:1–3, Priscilla and Aquila had been in Rome and had to leave when the emperor Claudius expelled the Jews from Rome. They left and went to Greece, where they met Paul and worked with him. By the time Paul wrote Romans, they had returned to Rome.

The secular historian Suetonius says that the emperor Claudius expelled the Jews from Rome because someone by the name of "Chrestus" was causing continuous disturbances.[1] *Chrestus* is the Latin spelling of *Christ*. It is quite possible that Suetonius didn't really understand the situation. Probably, non-Christian Jews and Jewish Christians like Priscilla and Aquila became involved in public disputes about Christ. And since emperors didn't like anything to rock the boat, Claudius just kicked all the Jews—Christian and non-Christian—out of Rome. Later, when Nero became emperor, he allowed the Jews back in. That's probably when Priscilla and Aquila returned.

These events might explain some of the tensions in the church at Rome. Imagine what might have happened if Jewish Christians had started the church in Rome and were leading it when they were kicked out of Rome with all the other Jews. The church then would probably have become primarily a Gentile Christian church with Gentile Christian leaders. (It seems that when Paul wrote the book of Romans, the majority of the church was made up of Gentile Christians; see Romans 11.) Then, when the original Jewish Christian leaders returned, there could well have been tension between them and the Gentile Christians who had become the church's leaders.

In the next chapter we turn to this issue of Jew and Gentile, and Paul's approach to it in Romans.

---

1. See *The Twelve Caesars,* "Claudius," Section 25.

CHAPTER 2

Jew and Gentile

No matter where or when one lives, the world seems to get divided into contrasting categories of people, with at least some degree of hostility between the two. It could be black versus white, young versus old, capitalist versus communist, east versus west, gay versus straight, Christian versus Muslim, Israeli versus Palestinian, or Republican versus Democrat—and I'm sure you could add a lot more to the list. People always seem to divide the human world into different groups, with preference given to their own group.

When Paul grew up in the first-century world, the division he knew best was the one between Jew and Gentile, and there was a significant level of hostility between the two. In Paul's later life he could speak of a "barrier" or "dividing wall of hostility" that stood between Jew and Gentile (Ephesians 2:14). It isn't hard to find rhetoric from the first century that confirms the existence of such a wall.

In the *Mishnah,* which was written about A.D. 190 but presents the tradition that had been passed on orally by the rabbis over a period of centuries, Gentiles don't come out all that well. For example, in Gittin 2:5 we read, "All are qualified to bring a bill of divorce excepting a deaf-mute, an imbecile, a minor, a blind man, or a Gentile."[1] The Jews considered Gentiles unclean, and they weren't allowed to eat with them. We see this within the New Testament itself in Peter's comment when he addresses Cornelius and his household: " 'You are well aware that it is against our law for a Jew to associate with a Gentile or visit him' " (Acts 10:28). In fact, some Jews interpreted their food laws as being a reminder that Jews were not to associate with unclean people such as Gentiles.[2]

On the other side of the coin, Gentile writings contain a lot of anti-Jewish rhetoric and rumor. The Roman historian Tacitus taught that Jews were kicked out of Egypt at the time of the Exodus because they had a disease that horribly disfigured the body. He said that in his time (late first century) the Jews taught and practiced all the things that all other peoples would consider the most perverse, disgusting, and degraded.[3] In *Against Apion,* Josephus tried to dispel the rumors that the anti-Jewish writer Apion had started by attributing horrible practices to the Jews. One of the most outrageous was that every year on the Day of Atonement the Jews kidnapped a Gentile whom they fattened with sumptuous feasts and, on the next Day of Atonement, sacrificed and ate.

Such hostility was not the rule everywhere. Many Jews and Gentiles co-existed with mutual goodwill. But often there was an undercurrent of suspicion that was fueled by rumors and innuendoes. And Paul grew up in the middle of this, with a foot in both the Jewish and Gentile worlds.

Paul's mission to the Gentiles

Paul, of course, was a Jew. He identified himself as a Jew throughout his life. At some point in his youth, he went to Jerusalem to study the strict form of Judaism practiced by the Pharisees. Even long after he accepted Jesus as his Savior, Lord, and Messiah, he still made it clear that he was a Jew. Notice the pedigree he claimed in Philippians 3:5, 6: "circumcised on the eighth day, of the people of Israel, of the tribe of Benjamin, a Hebrew of Hebrews; in regard to the law, a Pharisee; as for zeal, persecuting the church."

In Romans 9:1–4, he showed how important his people were to him even after his conversion: "I speak the truth in Christ—I am not lying, my conscience confirms it in the Holy Spirit—I have great sorrow and unceasing anguish in my heart. For I could wish that I myself were cursed and cut off from Christ for the sake of my brothers, those of my own race, the people of Israel."

And in Romans 11:1, he asked if God had rejected His people, and he answered his question by affirming that he himself was a Jew: "I ask then: Did God reject his people? Absolutely not! I am an Israelite myself, a descendant of Abraham, from the tribe of Benjamin."[4] So, there can be no question about Paul's Jewishness.

On the other hand, Paul grew up with at least one of his feet partially in the Gentile world as well. He was born in Tarsus, a Gentile city in Cilicia (Acts 21:39; 22:3). That city had an amphitheater where all the Greek sporting events were held, and Paul seems to have been familiar with that world. Whereas Jesus told stories about farmers going out to sow grain and fishermen with their nets, Paul used analogies about boxing matches and track meets (see 1 Corinthians 9:24–27; Philippians 3:13, 14). We don't know how or when he became a Roman citizen, but the book of Acts suggests that he took pride in the fact that he was one (see Acts 16:37; 22:25–29). He seemed to enjoy letting authorities who mistreated him know that they had mistreated a Roman citizen.

God chose this intense person who had familiarity with both the Jewish and Gentile worlds to be His chosen instrument to break down the wall between them and bring the two together. This is really what the incident on the road to Damascus was all about. We usually think of this as Paul's conversion to Christianity, but it is much more his call, or commission, to become the apostle to the Gentiles. This story is so important that it is told three times in the book of Acts, in chapters 9, 22, and 26. Paul's mission to the Gentiles is emphasized in each retelling. In Acts 9:15, 16, Ananias is told to go and meet Paul in spite of the rumors he has heard about him. God says, " 'Go! This man is my chosen instrument to carry my name before the Gentiles and their kings and before the people of Israel.' " In Acts 22:21, the Lord tells Paul, " ' "Go; I will send you far away to the Gentiles." ' " And in Acts 26:17, 18, He assures, " ' "I will rescue you from your own people and from the Gentiles. I am sending you to them to open their eyes and turn them from darkness to light, and from the power of Satan to God, so that they may receive forgiveness of sins and a place among those who are sanctified by faith in me." ' "

In both Galatians and Romans, Paul identified himself as an apostle to the Gentiles (Galatians 1:16; 2:1; Romans 11:13; 15:16). His specific mission was to bring the gospel to the Gentiles and to bring Jew and Gentile together. His approach to this task was multidimensional. One dimension was evangelistic, another was political, and yet another was theological.

Before we examine each of these aspects of Paul's ministry, we should say a word about the very notion of his being an apostle. According to Acts 1:21, an apostle had to have been with Jesus and had to have been a witness to His resurrection. It would have been easy for Paul's opponents to discredit his apostleship by pointing to the chronology. He was still persecuting Christians long after Jesus' ascension; how then could he satisfy the criteria for being an apostle?

Paul's answer was that the risen Jesus had appeared to him on the road to Damascus to commission him as an apostle with a special purpose—an apostle to the Gentiles. He admitted that this appearance didn't come at the right time; he was as one "abnormally born" (1 Corinthians 15:8), a term that could refer to either a premature or post-mature birth. But even though Paul's commission didn't come at the same time as that of the others, Christ's appearance to him was no less real than what the other apostles had experienced. Note what he wrote in 1 Corinthians 15:3–8:

> For what I received I passed on to you as of first importance: that Christ died for our sins according to the Scriptures, that he was buried, that he was raised on the third day

according to the Scriptures, and that he appeared to Peter, and then to the Twelve. After that, he appeared to more than five hundred of the brothers at the same time, most of whom are still living, though some have fallen asleep. Then he appeared to James, then to all the apostles, and last of all he appeared to me also, as to one abnormally born.

Paul, the evangelizing apostle

The most obvious badge of Paul's apostleship to the Gentiles was his evangelistic preaching among them. He traveled throughout Asia Minor and Europe preaching the gospel in town after town, often suffering beatings and imprisonment. In fact, he can say, "From Jerusalem all the way around to Illyricum, I have fully proclaimed the gospel of Christ" (Romans 15:19).

We know of Paul's evangelistic ministry both from the book of Acts, which outlines his missionary travels, and from his letters, which tell of his preaching to various congregations—and of his continuing to stay in touch by writing to them. He was a pastor as well as an evangelistic preacher, so he wanted to know how his converts were growing in their walk with God.

Often when Paul entered a city, his first converts came from a group of people called "God fearers." These were Gentiles who had been attracted to the Jewish religion by its monotheism and high ethical ideals but who had not actually become Jewish converts. These were people who were dissatisfied with pagan religion and were therefore ripe for the gospel. (See Acts 17:4, for example.) Since this is the most obvious aspect of Paul's ministry to the Gentiles, it needs the least attention.

Paul, the political apostle

Paul was a political apostle to the Gentiles. By "political" I'm not referring to secular politics, but the process of working within the organizational structures of the church. Paul not only took the gospel to the Gentiles through his preaching, but he also worked for the inclusion of Gentiles through the processes of church organization.

One way he did this was by participating in the church council held in Jerusalem around A.D. 49.

We have two accounts of this council, one given by Luke in Acts 15 and the other by Paul in Galatians 2. Although a few elements in the two accounts don't seem to correlate, the essential issue and decision are clear in both. The controversy began when some Christians came to Antioch and challenged Paul's practice of baptizing uncircumcised Gentiles (Acts 15:1; Galatians 2:4). Both accounts agree that the apostles' decision supported Paul's practice of baptizing Gentiles without demanding circumcision. In Galatians, Paul adds that he and Barnabas took an actual uncircumcised Christian, Titus, as exhibit A, to show what a Gentile Christian looked like. Titus wasn't compelled to be circumcised.

This conference had a significant impact on the early church, and Paul's participation was crucial to the outcome. The real issue was whether people had to become Jews before they could become Christians. In other words, it was whether the Christian faith was open to all or was open only to Jews. Paul's opponents in the church would have allowed Gentiles to join the church, but only if they became Jews. So, if Paul's opponents had won, the gospel would have been only for Jews. In essence, Gentiles would have had to convert to Judaism before their inclusion in the body of Christ.

It was not only by Paul's participation in the church council, however, that he sought to open the way for Jews and Gentiles to come together within the church. The collection that he took up from the Gentiles for the poor saints in Jerusalem was a political, or practical, attempt to bring the two sides—Jew and Gentile— together in Christ. According to Paul, he had been asked to do this at the Jerusalem Council (see Galatians 2:10). But he also indicates that he was anxious to do it.

The theological basis for the collection is seen in the following statement: "Macedonia and Achaia were pleased to make a contribution for the poor among the saints in Jerusalem. They were pleased to do it, and indeed they owe it to them. For if the Gentiles have shared in the Jews' spiritual blessings, they owe it to the Jews to share with them their material blessings" (Romans 15:26–28).

The spiritual blessing of the gospel originated with the Jews. But the Jews in Jerusalem, including the Jewish Christians, were poor, whereas the Gentiles to whom Paul preached in the cities of the Roman Empire were much more affluent. This mutual sharing of blessings was a visible symbol of the new unity that Jews and Gentiles found in Christ. Its importance for Paul can be seen in 2 Corinthians 8 and 9, where he urges the Corinthians to give to this cause, and in his willingness to travel all the way to Jerusalem from Corinth himself to take this collection to the poor saints when he wanted to go in the opposite direction, to Rome.

Paul knew that Christianity could have easily divided into two communities, a Jewish Christian church and a Gentile Christian church. His conviction that God desired the church to be one church in which both Jew and Gentile lived together in peace drove him to work politically as the apostle to the Gentiles.

Paul, the theological apostle to the Gentiles

Finally, Paul worked as a theologian to think through the message of salvation for all, both Jew and Gentile. Later in this volume we will explore his teaching of righteousness by faith, or salvation by grace through faith. We usually think of this doctrine as having to do with personal salvation, with the essential question being, "How can I be saved?" However, even though this is a very important part of the discussion for Paul, it isn't really what the doctrine of salvation by faith is all about. Paul is even more concerned with a broader question: How can God save both Jew and Gentile? The doctrine of justification by faith puts all humans on the same footing and therefore enables all to be included equally in God's grace.

All have sinned and fallen short of the glory of God, but all have also been called by God's grace. If salvation is based on God's grace rather than on human effort or achievement, then God is an equal-opportunity Savior. The words *every* and *all* are two of the most important theological terms in Romans. The real thesis sentence of the book is found in chapter 1:16: "I am not ashamed of the gospel, because it is the power of God for the salvation of everyone who believes: first for the Jew, then for the Gentile." The gospel is for everyone, Jew and Gentile. This universality of the gospel message for everyone drives Paul's theological thinking. If we consider only the question of personal salvation, we misunderstand the real center of Paul's message. The fact that God grants salvation by grace through faith apart from works of law means that it is His purpose to have "mercy on them all" (Romans 11:32).

Paul's theology has practical implications for Christian behavior and for missionary strategy. Regarding personal behavior, if God's purpose is to have mercy on all, then Christians ought to live a life of mercy—living, as far as it depends on the believer, at peace with all people (Romans 12:18). Christians are to welcome each other even when they disagree about particular practices and standards (Romans 15:7). God's grace is a model for our graciousness.

Regarding missionary strategy, Paul's theology means that he will become all things to all people in order to save some (1 Corinthians 9:19–23). To the Jew he will become like the Jew, although he won't really be under the law. To the Gentile he will be as a Gentile, although he'll always remember that he's bound to the law of Christ. This might lead some to think that Paul is inconsistent, but his apparent inconsistency is part of a broader faithfulness to the principle that he is to work for all people. So, for example, at the Jerusalem council he didn't give in for a second to those who demanded Titus's circumcision (Galatians 2:1–5). Yet when Timothy joined Paul toward the beginning of the second missionary journey, Paul had him circumcised rather than let him be a stumbling block to the Jews (Acts 16:1–3). These differing decisions might seem inconsistent, but they both are rooted in Paul's overall message of mercy for all.

So in Paul we see a multidimensional ministry with one major focus. God has a new plan: to bring both Jew and Gentile into a new community in which all the walls of hostility between them will be broken down and both can live together in God's community of peace.

---

1. Herbert Danby, *The Mishnah* (Oxford: Oxford University Press, 1933), 308.

2. See, for example, the Letter of Aristeas, 139–142.

3. Tacitus, *Histories,* book 5.

4. The words "absolutely not" in this passage and throughout this book are the author's own translation of this expression.—Ed.

CHAPTER

All Have Sinned

The book of Romans begins well. At least the first seventeen verses begin well. They culminate in the good news that God's righteousness has been revealed. *Righteousness* is certainly not a word we use every day in ordinary conversation, but it sounds like something positive. We'll spend some time in the next chapter examining what this righteousness is all about.

After the seventeen verses that lead to the revelation of God's righteousness, however, Paul changes the tone of the letter. He moves in a direction that doesn't seem so positive, which, in fact, sounds downright negative. Romans 1:18–3:20 talks about the revelation of God's wrath. This hardly sounds like good news! Most of us would just as soon forget about God's wrath. Haven't we gotten beyond all that "sinners in the hands of an angry God" stuff? But for Paul, the message of good news includes a rather lengthy discussion of God's wrath.

Let's start with the first few verses, which lead us to the revelation of righteousness. After that we'll have to follow Paul and spend some time thinking about God's wrath.

The revelation of righteousness

In our letters we leave the sender's name at the end, but in the

Greco-Roman world, letters started out with the name of the sender, followed by the name of the recipient, and then usually the word *Greetings.* So, Paul begins his letter with his name. But, stepping outside the customary form, he adds a few words about who he is. He's a servant, or slave, of Christ Jesus; he is called to be an apostle; and he's set apart for the gospel. He then expands the typical letter opening even further by giving a brief description of this gospel. It's the message prophesied in the Scriptures (for Paul, that meant the Old Testament), and it's about Jesus Christ, who was declared to be the Son of God by His resurrection from the dead.

Paul then adds that his mission is to call the Gentiles to the "obedience that comes from faith" (Romans 1:5). This concept is so important to him that he brackets the whole letter with it—we find it again in Romans 15:18, although Paul doesn't specifically mention faith here. So, at the beginning and the end of the letter, Paul makes his mission clear: God wants the Gentiles to come to obey Him by having faith.

After six verses Paul finally gets to the second part of the letter, which usually came after only a word or two. The recipients addressed in the letter are "all in Rome who are loved by God and called to be saints" (Romans 1:7). For Paul, the word *saints* didn't mean people in a cathedral's stained-glass window, but all those called by God and set apart for His service.

When Paul comes to the "greetings" line (the latter part of verse 7), he plays on it by using the word *grace* instead. The two words sound much alike, and *grace* was the most important term in Paul's theological vocabulary, so it makes sense that he would use it for his greetings. Other Christian letter writers did the same.

In verses 8–15, Paul speaks of his desire to visit the church in Rome, as we have noted in the previous two chapters. In verses 16 and 17, he comes to the thesis sentence of the letter. He is writing about the revelation of God's righteousness, a righteousness that comes from God and is attained on the basis of faith from beginning to end. He quotes Habakkuk 2:4 to make his point. This righteousness results in salvation and is for *all* human beings, both Jew and

Gentile. At this point, however, Paul doesn't explain the meaning of this righteousness. He'll do that in the latter part of chapter 3, and we'll wait until the next chapter for that discussion.

The revelation of wrath

As soon as Paul gets the idea of the revelation of righteousness out of his pen, he turns to the revelation of wrath. In verse 18, he says that God's wrath "is being revealed from heaven against all the godlessness and wickedness" of human beings. This raises two questions: What is God's wrath? and Who are these godless and wicked human beings?

Paul makes the nature of God's wrath clear in the verses that follow. His use of the term may not be quite the same as that of other biblical writers; for him, God's wrath is the other side of the coin of His decision to grant freedom to human beings. God gives human beings the freedom to accept or reject Him, but their actions have consequences. God's wrath is His letting people live with the consequences of their choices. He hands them over or "[gives] them over" to their own choices and actions (verse 24). God's wrath is not His *direct action against* human beings, it is rather His *turning them over* to the results of their own choices. To paraphrase an old adage, He lets them sleep in the bed they've made for themselves.

The word that Paul used that's translated as God giving them over is an interesting word. It is used in several important ways in the New Testament. It can refer to written or oral tradition that is handed over to another person, to the giving over of one's self in surrender as in war, to entrusting an object to another person, or to giving another person over to authorities for arrest or execution.

Paul uses the term three times in just a few verses in the context of God's wrath to speak of His handing over or giving people over to their own devices. All three such uses occur within Romans 1:24–32:

Therefore God *gave them over* in the sinful desires of their hearts to sexual impurity for the degrading of their bodies with one another. They exchanged the truth of God for a lie, and worshiped and served created things rather than the Creator— who is forever praised. Amen.

Because of this, God *gave them over* to shameful lusts. Even their women exchanged natural relations for unnatural ones. In the same way the men also abandoned natural relations with women and were inflamed with lust for one another. Men committed indecent acts with other men, and received in themselves the due penalty for their perversion.

Furthermore, since they did not think it worthwhile to retain the knowledge of God, he *gave them over* to a depraved mind, to do what ought not to be done. They have become filled with every kind of wickedness, evil, greed and depravity. They are full of envy, murder, strife, deceit and malice. They are gossips, slanderers, God-haters, insolent, arrogant and boastful; they invent ways of doing evil; they disobey their parents; they are senseless, faithless, heartless, ruthless. Although they know God's righteous decree that those who do such things deserve death, they not only continue to do these very things but also approve of those who practice them (emphasis added).

Three times Paul emphasizes that God "gave them over" to their evil choices. This is not God's active punishment of human beings for their sins. Rather, it is Him passively allowing them to reap the results of turning their backs on Him and His ways.

Yet Paul does point out another aspect of God's wrath as well. A day of final judgment will come, "because of your stubbornness and your unrepentant heart, you are storing up wrath against yourself for the day of God's wrath, when his righteous judgment will be revealed" (Romans 2:5, 6).

This revelation of God's wrath, however, is not His final word. God values freedom, so He leaves people to the consequences of their decisions. But He loves human beings even more, so He intervenes with His grace through Jesus Christ to offer forgiveness and salvation in spite of people's choices. Twice in the subsequent chapters of Romans Paul uses the term *gave over* in a positive way. In those places he says that in spite of human wickedness, God *gave Jesus over* for our sins and for our deliverance. But that gets us too far ahead of ourselves in the story. We'll come to those texts later.

Gentile—and Jewish—sin

Now to the second question: who are these wicked people? The sins listed in the passage quoted above, Romans 1:24–32, are the sins that the Jews regularly condemned in the Gentile world. Jewish invectives against the Gentiles usually focused on their sexual immorality and their idolatry. Of course, in the Greco-Roman world, these two usually went together, since pagan temples housed a good share of the prostitutes. Any Jew reading the last half of the first chapter of Romans would have said, "Right on, Brother Paul. You're really hitting the nail on the head now. How insightful of you to call sin by its right name and condemn those Gentile sinners. They certainly deserve it!"

Paul's description of the Gentile world was accurate. You only have to read the descriptions that Roman historians and moralists gave of the banquets in homes, temples, and palaces to see that such activities were prevalent in first-century Greco-Roman culture.

But does Paul ever turn the tables in chapter 2! Right when the Jews would be shouting their "Amens," Paul turns his guns on them. He says, "You, therefore, have no excuse, you who pass judgment on someone else, for at whatever point you judge the other, you are condemning yourself, because you who pass judgment do the same things" (Romans 2:1, 2).

For Paul, judging others for their sins is just as bad as the sins they are committing. God alone is Judge. To judge others is to usurp God's role and is therefore a kind of blasphemy. In addition, Jews often ended up committing in secret the same sins that the Gentiles did openly. So, in chapter 2, Paul is just as hard on the Jews as he was on the Gentiles in chapter 1. Notice what he says in Romans 2:17–24:

Now you, if you call yourself a Jew; if you rely on the law and brag about your relationship to God; if you know his will and approve of what is superior because you are instructed by the law; if you are convinced that you are a guide for the blind, a light for those who are in the dark, an instructor of the foolish, a teacher of infants, because you have in the law the embodiment of knowledge and truth—you, then, who teach others, do you not teach yourself? You who preach against stealing, do you steal? You who say that people should not commit adultery, do you commit adultery? You who abhor idols, do you rob temples? You who brag about the law, do you dishonor God by breaking the law? As it is written: "God's name is blasphemed among the Gentiles because of you."[1]

Paul says the Jews are such poor witnesses that they give God a bad name among the Gentiles.

Universal sin

Paul states the basic principle in Romans 2:11: God shows no partiality. His wrath is equal opportunity, all the way. Jews and Gentiles are both sinners. This leads to the conclusion in Romans 3 that no one is righteous. Paul says, "We have already made the charge that Jews and Gentiles alike are all under sin" (Romans 3:9).

After saying this, Paul does something interesting. He goes back to the Old Testament and puts together a whole string of texts (mostly from Psalms), that support his point. In doing so, he picks all the harshest denunciations of human sinfulness that he can find. The passages included in his array of texts, in order of occurrence, are Psalm 14:1–3; Psalm 53:1–3; Ecclesiastes 7:20; Psalm 5:9; Psalm 140:3; Psalm 10:7; Isaiah 59:7, 8; and Psalm 36:1. Put all together, Paul's message seems pretty bleak:

"There is no one righteous, not even one;
   there is no one who understands,

30

no one who seeks God.
All have turned away,
  they have together become worthless;
there is no one who does good,
  not even one."
"Their throats are open graves;
  their tongues practice deceit."
"The poison of vipers is on their lips."
  "Their mouths are full of cursing and bitterness."
"Their feet are swift to shed blood;
  ruin and misery mark their ways,
and the way of peace they do not know."
  "There is no fear of God before their eyes" (Romans 3:10–18).

We might well be tempted to ask, "Paul, is it really all that bleak? Don't you want to qualify this a bit? You're going to discourage us all!" But at this point, Paul wants to paint the picture as bleakly as he can. He wants to make sure that no one goes away from this section of Romans saying, "He really gave it to those wicked people, and am I ever glad I'm not like that!" Remember the old car rental commercials that said, "Let Hertz put you in the driver's seat"? Paul wants to make sure we realize that he has put all of us in a seat—but it's not the driver's seat, it's the seat of the guilty. The bottom line is "there is no difference, for all have sinned and fall short of the glory of God" (Romans 3:22, 23).

Only by proving the universality of sin can Paul logically move to the all-inclusiveness of the free gift of salvation, which is his real concern. The message he wants to communicate is about righteousness, not wrath; grace, not the giving over of all people to wickedness. But his message makes sense only if he first lays the foundation of universal sin. Only if we are all in the same doomed boat of sinfulness can the same life raft of grace save us all.

Some peripheral issues

This section of Romans raises some issues that have caused extensive discussions, arguments, and debates. In most cases, however, Paul isn't discussing the issues that we like to debate, and therefore, it is dangerous for us to draw conclusions regarding these issues. For example, the question of natural law that Paul seems to raise in Romans 1:18–20 and 2:15, 16, has generated many debates. In these passages, Paul speaks of Gentiles who do by nature the things of the law. Is he here affirming a natural law that it sufficient for salvation apart from knowing Christ? Or is he referring to Gentiles who have come to know Christ and who therefore do the things the law requires because through the new covenant these things are now written in their hearts?

It is true that Seventh-day Adventists believe, on the basis of Ellen White's writings, that there will be people in God's kingdom who have never heard the name of Christ but have responded to God's voice in their hearts. But we don't have sufficient evidence to conclude with certainty that this is what Paul is addressing here. We have to remember that the subject in this section of Romans is not how people are saved, but the universality of sin. Paul may simply be pointing out that Gentiles do good things—that Jews don't have a monopoly on virtue. But his bottom line is still that all are sinners.

Another much debated issue is sexuality, especially homosexuality. Again, this is not Paul's topic. He doesn't address issues important to us, such as the difference between homosexual orientation and homosexual practice and how we should treat such a distinction. He is simply showing that the homosexual practice he sees in society is evidence of the sinfulness of the world.

Now that we have completed our examination of God's wrath and the universality of sin, we are prepared to move to the divine solution, the gracious good news of righteousness by faith.

---

1. The last sentence is based on Isaiah 52:5 and Ezekiel 36:22.

A Note on the Literary Features of Romans 1:29-31

Several literary devices come through in the original Greek of Romans 1:29–31 that are lost in translation. For example, Paul coupled together the Greek words for "envy" and "murder": *phthonou* and *phonou* (verse 29). He also grouped together three words that end with an *ia* sound: *adikia, poneria,* and *pleonexia,* which are translated "wickedness," "evil," and "greed" (verse 29). And in the original Greek, the words "foolish" and "faithless" are *asunetous* and *asunthetous* (verse 31). Paul also uses onomatopoeia—words that sound like what they mean. For example, the Greek term for people who gossip literally means "whisperers" (verse 29). When you pronounce the Greek original, *psithuristas,* you can hear the whispering!

Remember, Paul didn't write Romans with a pen in hand. According to Romans 16:22, he dictated it to a scribe named Tertius. This name means "third," and it probably indicates that the scribe was a slave, since slaves were often named just *First, Second, Third,* and so forth. You can almost hear Paul having fun with these words that sound alike and have alliteration as he rolls them off his tongue for Tertius to write down.

CHAPTER 4

Justified by Faith

In Romans 1:18, Paul spoke of God's wrath being revealed. But in Romans 3:21, he speaks of righteousness being revealed. We're moving from the problem to the solution. What is God's answer to the problem that all have sinned? It's the revelation of a righteousness that comes from Him, exists apart from the law, and comes by faith. This is the good news. But the fact that justification by faith is good news doesn't mean that it's always been a popular idea.

As I write this chapter, one of the persistent news items on TV has been the trial of a man who kidnapped, tortured, and brutally murdered a little child. He was convicted and sentenced to life imprisonment without the possibility of parole. Some were unhappy that he wasn't sentenced to death, but I haven't heard of anyone who thought the sentence was too harsh. No one would want this man free. Can you imagine someone with a small child having to live next door to him?

And can you imagine what an outrage it would be if a well-known, outstanding citizen came to the judge and said, "I'm willing to take this man's place and suffer his punishment. Send me to prison in his place and let him go free"? Would any judge take the volunteer substitute up on this offer? How would justice be served by acquitting a guilty man and letting him go free, even if someone else was willing to take on both the charge against him and his punishment?

According to the Old Testament, God would hardly be happy with such an arrangement: "Acquitting the guilty and condemning the innocent—the LORD detests them both" (Proverbs 17:15). Who wants to see a guilty person acquitted? So, it's hardly surprising that many people have questioned the notion of justification by faith that Paul presents in Romans 3:21–31. If the word *justification* is synonymous with acquittal in a court of law, how does it make sense that God acquits sinners freely by His grace (Romans 3:21–24)?

Such questions have led to theological debates both within Adventism and in the broader Christian community about the nature of justification. Is it purely a legal matter in which, on the basis of Jesus' substitution, sinners are declared righteous even though they aren't righteous? That kind of justification seems to be a legal fiction. On the other hand, some interpret justification as "making righteous." They say that when God justifies people, He actually changes them so they're no longer sinners. They aren't merely declared righteous, they *are* righteous!

What does *righteousness* mean?

Both of these positions probably oversimplify the issue of *justification* or *righteousness*. The term is both complex and rich. It is true that it comes from a legal context and is basically synonymous with acquittal. But before we decide what *righteousness* means, we need to understand four things.

First, confusion can arise over the translation of these terms. Several Greek words share a common root, *dik,* and all of them are translated in various ways in English. The adjective (*dikaios*) is translated as "just" or "righteous." The noun (*dikaiosynē*) can be translated "justice," "justification," or "righteousness." The verb (*dikaioō*) is sometimes translated "justify," "declare righteous," "pronounce righteous," or "make righteous."

Not only is there little consistency among the various Bible translations, but even within a given version these terms are translated differently. For example, Paul used the term *dikaiosynē* four times in Romans 3:21–31. The New International Version translates this term as "righteousness" in verses 21 and 22 and as "justice" in verses 25 and 26. The choices that translators make often reflect the theology they hold when they begin their work of translating.

Second, this complex of terms comes from the legal system of biblical times, which was quite different from the systems we have today. Our vision of justice is the blindfolded woman who holds the scales; we think of a judge as an objective deliberator who hands down unbiased decisions. In biblical times, however, the judges were much more actively involved in the lives of people they served. The judges were responsible for setting things right and working to vindicate the oppressed.

We see this in the Gospels when Jesus tells a story about an unjust judge (Luke 18:1–8). Jesus' point has to do with the complainant's persistence as a model for prayer, but the story also tells us something about the expectations people of that time held toward judges. In the story, the judge feared neither God nor human beings. A woman who had been wronged kept coming to him to find vindication against her adversary. The judge didn't care about justice, so he kept sending her away. But finally, because of her persistence, he gave in and vindicated her. Judges were expected to take action and go out and set the situation right. They didn't just sit on the bench and make decisions.

Third, the term *righteousness* has a rich Old Testament background that goes beyond the strictly legal setting. God's righteousness is His faithfulness to His covenant with His people. It refers to His never-ending, steadfast love that forgives and restores over and over again, even when people are unfaithful.

Fourth, *righteousness* isn't the only term Paul uses in this section to communicate the solution to the problem of human sin. There are other terms as well, such as *redemption* and *expiation* (also translated as "propitiation," "mercy seat," or "sacrifice of atonement"). All these terms were picture words in Paul's day. Unfortunately, we've lost the everyday images that these words would have automatically brought to the mind's eye of Paul's original hearers.

In view of these background items, how might Paul's first hearers have understood the notion of *righteousness*? They wouldn't have seen it as merely a legal term. Nor would they have seen it as an ethical term, as if it meant "behaviorally good." They probably would have thought, *Oh, God is like a judge who goes out and tries to set wrongs right.* They also would have thought of how often God had shown His faithfulness in the Old Testament. That's why Paul says that this righteousness was already testified to by the law and prophets (see Romans 3:21). In other words, Paul's hearers would have thought more metaphorically than we do.

God was neither declaring guilty people innocent nor making sinners instantaneously sinless. He was reaching out to people who had turned away from Him and was restoring them to a new, covenantal relationship with Him. For them, *righteousness* would have been a relational term. It meant being set right with God in a new, saving relationship in which God became Friend and Savior. Basically, in the biblical context, *righteousness* is not so much legal or behavioral as it is relational. Righteousness resulted when the judge helped restore broken relationships and set them right.

This concept was audacious, however, because Paul says that this new relationship, in which one is set right with God, can't come on the basis of human achievement. It is apart from law. By "law," Paul probably means the whole system of Judaism, but he certainly would have included the Ten Commandments. No human action—not even the keeping of the Ten Commandments or any other law—can commend us to God and bring about righteousness. That comes only by God's grace—His unearned acceptance. We can't earn it or take any credit for it. This is why all boasting "is excluded" (verse 27). No Christians can ever pat themselves on the back and say, "Look what I did to get myself righteous." Righteousness is a free gift of God.

We receive this free gift on the basis of faith, which, in this context, is a total commitment of trust in God. Bible scholars debate the meaning of the expression "faith of Jesus" in Romans 3:22

(KJV). Some say it means *faith in Jesus*. That's how the New International Version translates the phrase. Others say it means *Jesus' own faith* or *faithfulness*. But whichever is true, the text goes on to make it clear that it is for those who have faith or trust in God. To receive this free, gracious gift of righteousness, we must trust God. Faith, or total reliance on, trust in, and commitment to God, is the only appropriate response to His grace. But Christians are indebted to God even for this faith. Trusting God isn't a work that earns them righteousness; it is the recognition that nothing could ever earn them righteousness, and therefore, they must come to depend totally on God.

To summarize what we've covered so far: all humans have sinned and are hopelessly lost. God took the initiative of His own grace to reach out and save sinners by sending His Son, Jesus Christ, to die for them. The only appropriate response to this grace is total dependence on God, which rules out all boasting and recognizes that human beings can do nothing to earn their salvation.

Metaphors of atonement

Many theologians have tried to develop theories of the atonement that explain exactly how God saves us through Christ's death and resurrection—substitution, ransom, moral influence, and so forth. Paul hasn't given us a theory of atonement. Rather, he uses metaphors to help us picture what God has done for us. Every metaphor tells us something important, but none tells the whole story. That's true in this passage as well. Unfortunately, we've lost the pictures that stand behind these metaphors, pictures that would have been second nature to Paul's first readers.

As we've already noticed, *righteousness* is the most dominating metaphor in this passage. It presents a picture of God as a faithful judge who decisively goes out and sets things right by establishing a new relationship with hopeless sinners through Christ. But the picture of God isn't limited to that of a faithful judge. Paul also uses the metaphor of redemption (verse 24). This would have caused first-century Christians to think of a slave being set free. It happened all the time in their world. Slaves comprised about a third of the population, and many were being set free. Owners often decreed in their wills that at their death their slaves be set free. Other slaves were freed when someone was willing to put up the price to buy them and set them free. The freedmen became a large class in Roman society. Roman satirists in Paul's day decried the fact that many of these freedmen became wealthy and lived above their supposed status. Not only are we acquitted and set right as might happen in a court of law, but we are also set free as might happen in the slave market.

An additional metaphor is the term that the New International Version translates as "sacrifice of atonement" in Romans 3:25. The only other occurrence of this word in the New Testament is translated "mercy seat" (Hebrews 9:5, NRSV). This was its original meaning: the space above the ark of the covenant. But in Romans it probably means more than that. God presented Jesus as the Sacrifice. This is yet another metaphor, which suggests that just as sin was symbolically atoned for in the sacrifices in the temple, so Christ truly atones for our sins. The picture here is the temple and its sacrifices. Since none of us has ever gone to a temple and sacrificed a lamb, the metaphor probably doesn't mean as much to us as it did to the Romans.

What are these metaphors accomplishing? Paul isn't merely speaking as an abstract theologian here. He is speaking as a preacher and pastor. He is using illustrations that create pictures in the hearers' minds: as in a court, we have been acquitted; as in a slave market, we have been set free; and as in a temple, our sins have been atoned for by the blood of Christ Himself. We have often made these terms too abstract and have failed to see that Paul was writing as a pastor who was concerned for the spiritual well-being of those who would hear this letter read.

Righteousness for all

There is yet another audacious aspect to Paul's announcement of the revelation of God's righteousness. It is for *all* who believe; there is no distinction between Jew and Gentile (Romans 3:22). The Jews, however, believed that God had made a distinction. He had said as much in Exodus 8:22, 23. When He sent the plagues that traumatized the Egyptians, the Israelites were spared. God said this was to show that He made a distinction between Israel and the other nations. Now Paul is saying God doesn't make any distinctions. How can that be?

Paul answers that question by citing the central affirmation of the Jewish faith. If you go to a Jewish synagogue today, whatever the service is, you will hear the *Shema*. It is the recitation of Deuteronomy 6:4: "Hear, O Israel: The LORD our God, the LORD is one." Paul argues that if a person takes this central affirmation of Judaism seriously, God cannot be the God of the Jews only; He must also be "the God of Gentiles" (Romans 3:29). And if God is the God of both Jew and Gentile, and if both have sinned, and if His restoring righteousness is given freely at His own initiative by grace, then doesn't it make sense that He will deal the same way with both Jew and Gentile?[1]

So, the scope of this gift is as wide as it can be. It embraces all. The free gift is for everyone who responds appropriately with faith. As we have noted in chapter 2, righteousness by faith is not just a doctrine about how individuals are saved. Paul's mission is to bring Jew and Gentile together. We are all in the same boat of sin, and if we choose to put our faith in God, we will all be in the one boat of salvation. There are no distinctions between Jew and Gentile or between any other classes into which we can divide human beings. Righteousness is for all. In fact, this righteousness even goes beyond humans. Gods goal is cosmic. He is setting everything right in the whole universe.

We've already seen that this righteousness for all from God is "apart from law" (Romans 3:21). Paul repeats this again in verse 28: "We hold that a person is justified by faith apart from works prescribed by the law" (NRSV). No amount of obedience, good works, or achievement could ever commend us to God or earn our salvation. That might lead one to the conclusion that the law is therefore expendable—it is abolished. Paul knows that such a conclusion might be possible; therefore he asks the question at the end of this chapter, "Do we, then, nullify the law by this faith?" In the light of what he has said, we might not be surprised to hear that the answer would be "Yes!" But it isn't. In fact, it doesn't even come close. The answer is, "Absolutely not! Rather, we uphold the law" (Romans 3:31).[2]

Paul doesn't flesh this out until we get to chapters 6 and 7 of Romans. There he speaks to the issue of the continuing function of the law and the question of human behavior in light of the fact that salvation is a gift of God's grace alone. But he has already given us some clues in this chapter. He has already told us that the law makes us "conscious of sin" (verse 20). That doesn't solve the sin problem; it just shows that sin is there.

Another clue comes early in chapter 3. In the first few verses of the chapter, Paul raised a number of rhetorical questions, but he didn't answer them. One of the questions was, Why not say, Let's just do evil if good results because God's grace takes care of the evil? In other words, some people might possibly respond to Paul's doctrine of grace by living it up and sinning as they please because grace will take care of the sins anyway. Paul admits that wasn't just a theoretically possible conclusion from his teaching; some who listened to him actually claimed that this is what he was indeed teaching. Paul writes them off by saying, "Their condemnation is deserved" (verse 8). But in Romans 6 and 7, he will deal with the question in detail. We'll discuss that in a later chapter.

A story

Last Christmas all three of our grandsons were with us (at that point at the ages of five, four, and one). The space under the tree was overflowing with beautifully wrapped presents for each of them to open—so many, in fact, that they got bored before they finished. But one very simple little present excited the four- and five-year-olds more than many much nicer and more expensive gifts: rocket balloons. These are long, narrow balloons that you blow up and then let go so you can watch them fly. Rocket balloons didn't exist when I was a kid. We used to blow up regular balloons and let them go, but they didn't go very long or very far. Rocket balloons have such a narrow opening that they go and go and go. And to make them even more exciting, they have a whistle in the opening that provides sound effects.

In our house, we have the perfect spot for launching rocket balloons. Our entryway is two stories high and has a balcony on the second story. You can stand on the balcony and let the balloons fly all around and land in the entryway below.

The boys flew the rocket balloons for some time. But then one of the balloons hit the wall and—perhaps having some moisture on the outside—stuck to it. The balloon was too far out from the balcony for the boys to reach it. So my innovative grandsons ran downstairs and started trying to leap up and get it. But the balloon was stuck about twelve feet above the entryway floor. Imagine the two boys, the tallest just over forty inches tall, trying to leap up the twelve feet to get the balloon! Needless to say, it didn't work.

But they didn't give up. They went into the utility room and got a small ladder my wife uses to get into upper cupboards. It's barely three feet high. Three feet, plus forty inches, plus a little bit of reach still doesn't get close to twelve feet. After a while they recognized they weren't going to reach the balloon with that ladder, so they decided they had seen a bigger ladder in the garage and they would get that one. Then, just as they were folding the little ladder so they could go get the big one, the balloon—apparently having dried out—fell down on their heads.

There were two totally different reactions. One boy jumped up and down for joy and shouted, "We have it!" The other broke into tears and said, "But I wanted us to do it all by ourselves!"

Paul's good news is that God has freely poured out His grace on us and saved us. The appropriate response is to shout for joy because it's something we could never do all by ourselves.

---

1. Paul will continue this theme in more detail in Romans 9–11, where he will show that God's inclusion of the Gentiles in no way nullifies His promise of faithfulness to the Jews.

2. The words "absolutely not" in this passage and throughout this book are the author's own translation of this expression. —Ed.

CHAPTER 5

Justification, Law, and Abraham

At this point in Paul's letter he has set forth his basic proposal. God's wrath is revealed in universal sin, and God's righteousness is revealed in the free gift of grace offered to all people on the basis of faith apart from the law. These could have been fighting words to some of Paul's Jewish readers for two reasons. First, they might have seen him as undermining the law and opening the way for a relativistic free-for-all in which everyone felt free to do as they pleased. As we already saw, Paul admitted that some people accused him of teaching exactly that (see Romans 3:8).

Second, Jewish readers might have thought Paul was undermining the promise God had made to their ancestors. Didn't the covenant indicate that God had chosen the Jews to be a special people? Now Paul was saying that God doesn't play favorites. He regards everyone the same way. All are sinners in need of His grace. Both of these points certainly would have at least raised eyebrows and might even have produced some theological fistfights.

Paul understands his readers. He knows what they're thinking. So, as good pastors do, he stops to provide an example both to illustrate and to bolster the points he has made. And what better example could there be than Abraham? He was the father of the Jews. If Paul could show that Abraham's experience proved what he was saying, Paul would go a long way toward breaking down the opposition to these two controversial points.

The importance of Abraham

Even in Old Testament times, Abraham was considered the model to look at with regard to righteousness. Notice Isaiah 51:1, 2:

"Listen to me, you who pursue righteousness
    and who seek the LORD:
Look to the rock from which you were cut
    and to the quarry from which you were hewn;
look to Abraham, your father,
    and to Sarah, who gave you birth.
When I called him he was but one,
    and I blessed him and made him many."

The great prophet Isaiah says that if you want to pursue righteousness and seek the Lord, you need to look to Abraham, the father of the Jews. He's the one who will show you how to be righteous.

The noninspired books written in the time between the Old and New Testaments also recognize Abraham's importance as well. In the book called the Wisdom of Ben Sirach, or Ecclesiasticus (not to be confused with the canonical book Ecclesiastes), we read,

Abraham was the great father of a multitude of nations,
    and no one has been found like him in glory.
He kept the law of the Most High,
    and entered into a covenant with him (44:19, 20, NRSV).

Abraham was seen as the one who kept the law, which made the Jews regard him as a great example. Notice that in this book he is seen as the father of other nations too.

The New Testament also upholds Abraham as an example. Matthew traces Jesus' genealogy to Abraham (Matthew 1). He wants to show that Jesus' ancestry goes back to the father of the Jews. The fact that Jesus is a legitimate heir of Abraham gives Him credibility. And in Hebrews 11, in the list of those who are great examples of faith, Abraham gets more space than anyone else does. So, from the Old Testament through the period between the Testaments, right down to New Testament, Abraham is seen as the father of the Jews and the example who inspires them to obey God. If Paul can show that Abraham's example actually supports what he is saying, then he will have proved his point. And Paul does just that. He finds two texts about Abraham in the book of Genesis that speak to both of the controversial points with which we began this chapter.

Abraham and Genesis

Paul's two passages are Genesis 15:6 and 17:5. The first speaks to the issue of salvation by faith and not works, and the second speaks to the issue of the universality of God's grace. Paul shows that on both issues, Abraham is on his side.

The first passage is quoted in Romans 4:3. It quotes Genesis 15:6, which says, "Abram [Abraham] believed the LORD, and he credited it to him as righteousness." This, of course, could also be translated as "Abram trusted God" or "had faith in God." Paul uses this passage to emphasize that something credited to you isn't something you've earned. So, Genesis says Abraham didn't earn his righteousness; it was given as a gift, based on his faith in God. It was because Abraham had faith in God that this righteousness was given to him. Thus, Abraham became the perfect example of righteousness by faith.

But there's another point to be made here as well. The incident recorded in Genesis 15:6 occurred before Abraham was circumcised (Romans 4:9–12). Therefore, his righteousness could hardly be based on circumcision. And since circumcision was the sign that one was a Jew, Abraham's righteousness couldn't have been based on his Judaism. So, if Abraham is the prime example of righteousness, then we must conclude that righteousness is a gift credited on the basis of faith. It isn't the result either of law-keeping or of being a Jew. This is just what Paul had said in chapter 3. Now he has Abraham on his side as well!

Paul quotes the second passage, Genesis 17:5, in Romans 4:17: " 'I have made you a father of many nations.' " When you read this, keep in mind that the Greek word translated "nations" can also be translated "Gentiles." Abraham is not only the father of the Jews; he's also the father of the Gentiles. The Jews of Paul's day believed this, but they hadn't really recognized all the implications. Paul makes sure they do. If Abraham is the example of righteousness and is also the father of the Gentiles, then God's salvation can hardly be limited to the Jews.

The Jews saw themselves as heirs of the promises made to Abraham. Paul affirms that they are. But they aren't the only heirs. The Gentiles are heirs of the promise as well. Both stand on equal footing, and both are saved in the same way—by putting their trust in God.

This message in Romans rules out the doctrine of dispensationalism that many evangelical Christians hold today. The dispensationalists say that God has had different methods of salvation in different eras of earth's history. There was an old covenant dispensation in which people were saved by obedience to the law. But Christ ushered in a new covenant dispensation of grace. In this new covenant of grace, the law is abolished and is no longer valid.

There are two problems with this view. First, Paul teaches in Romans that everyone is saved in the same way. In the time of Abraham as in the time of Paul, people were saved by putting their trust in God. Righteousness was always a gift of God's grace. The law was never intended to save us. It reveals sin, but only God can save us.

In Romans 3:25, 26, Paul says that God passed over former sins with a view to demonstrating His righteousness at the present time. This doesn't mean that God ignored those sins or didn't care about them. It means that He was waiting for the solution to the sin problem in Jesus Christ. All people in all eras have been saved in the same way—by trusting in God's grace.

The second problem with the dispensationalist view is that the new covenant doesn't abolish the law. Passages that speak of the new covenant—such as Jeremiah 31:31–34 and Hebrews 8:8–12, which quotes the Jeremiah passage—don't speak of doing away with the law, but of changing its location. In the new covenant, the law is no longer an external code; it is written on the heart. It is internalized. To have the law written on the heart and internalized is not to ignore it or to break it, but to live according to it—not because we have to, but because we want to.

It's one thing to say, "I sure wish I could steal my neighbor's lawn mower, but the law says I'm not supposed to steal, so I guess I won't. What a bummer!" It's quite another to have so much love for my neighbor that I wouldn't want to steal his lawn mower or anything else that belongs to him. Thus, the new covenant's internalization of the law does just the opposite of abolishing it. That is precisely what Paul means in Romans 3:31: "Do we, then, nullify the law by this faith? [Absolutely not!] Not at all! Rather, we uphold the law."

So, for Paul, everyone is saved in the same way—by trusting a God of grace. Abraham is exhibit A of this truth.

Other lessons from Abraham

While the two points Paul made by quoting Genesis 15:6 and 17:5—that Abraham was saved by faith, and that he is the father of the Gentiles as well as of the Jews—are Paul's central points in this chapter, he draws several other lessons from Abraham as well. We see these in the final verses of chapter 4:

> Against all hope, Abraham in hope believed and so became the father of many nations, just as it had been said to him, "So shall your offspring be." Without weakening in his faith, he faced the fact that his body was as good as dead—since he was about a hundred years old—and that Sarah's womb was also dead. Yet he did not waver through unbelief regarding the promise of God, but was strengthened in his faith and gave glory to God, being fully persuaded that God

47

had power to do what he had promised. This is why "it was credited to him as righteousness." The words "it was credited to him" were written not for him alone, but also for us, to whom God will credit righteousness—for us who believe in him who raised Jesus our Lord from the dead. He was delivered over to death for our sins and was raised to life for our justification (verses 18–25).

Paul uses Abraham's example to show us something about the nature of faith. Having faith means trusting God even when the odds seem to be against what He says. Abraham was an old man with a body about as good as dead when God told him he would be a father to many nations. While Abraham's body was weak, his faith was strong. It is this kind of strong faith that trusts God even when His promise seems so doubtful.

This is exactly the situation that many of us are in with regard to salvation. We find it hard to accept the news that we are saved by God's grace in spite of ourselves. We think God's acceptance may apply to others, but we know ourselves too well to believe it means us too. However, according to Paul, God's promises weren't written just for Abraham, they were written for you and me too. Christ was delivered over to death for *our* sins and was raised for *our* justification!

We find in Romans 4:25 the same word that we noted three times in Romans 1:18–28. There the word was used to show the nature of God's wrath—God *gave over* or *handed over* the sinners to their wickedness. But God couldn't let wrath be the last word. Therefore, He *delivered* Jesus *up* or *handed* Him *over* for our sins and then raised Him for our justification.

Preparing the way

Now for some observations about the book of Romans at large. In Romans 4, Paul emphasizes the strength of Abraham's faith in contrast to weak faith. He may be doing that as a foretaste of something he will focus on toward the end of the letter. It might be helpful to notice that this is only one of several elements in these first few chapters that anticipate his discussion in Romans 14 and 15.

As we will see toward the end of this book, there is controversy over how the various sections of Romans are related to each other. Just about everyone recognizes that Romans easily divides into three parts: chapters 1–8, 9–11, and 12–16. The question is how these three parts are related to each other. For now, let's focus on just the first and the last sections.

Some scholars have seen virtually no relationship between the first and the last sections of Romans. They say that in chapters 1–8, Paul sets forth his basic theological message, and in chapters 12–16, he gives the kind of traditional ethical thinking that you find at the end of most of the philosophical essays written by Greco-Roman writers. This section, they think, isn't really related to the theological message of Romans; it's more or less tacked on as an appendix that can be read without regard to the rest of the letter. Some have even gone so far as to say that chapters 12–16 are more or less inconsistent with the early part of the letter because they focus on behavior, which contradicts Paul's early message of grace.

Others hold that the third section of Romans is really the climax of the letter, toward which Paul has been heading from the very beginning. He's concerned not just about what people believe, but also about how they act, especially how they treat each other. God's grace toward us should lead us to treat others with grace. Paul is very concerned about the Romans' quibbling over matters such as food, and he's trying to lead them to a new unity in Christ. So, the first section of Romans, chapters 1–8, is laying the groundwork for Paul's very real pastoral concern about what is happening in Rome, which is what he addresses in chapters 14 and 15.

There is very good evidence that this second position is correct, for there are various passages in the early chapters of Romans that seem to anticipate and prepare the way for what Paul says in chapters 14 and 15 when he gets down to the specific problems in Rome.

For instance, Paul begins chapter 2 by saying, "You, therefore, have no excuse, you who pass judgment on someone else, for at whatever point you judge the other, you are condemning yourself" (verse 1). When Paul gets to Romans 14, we find that this is exactly what the Roman believers are doing—they're judging each other. Thus, Paul says there, "You, then, why do you judge your brother? Or why do you look down on your brother? For we will all stand before God's judgment seat" (verses 10, 11). And in verse 13, Paul adds, "Therefore let us stop passing judgment on one another." It appears that the Romans have a problem with judging, and as early as chapter 2, Paul is preparing the way for what he will say later about this problem.

Another of these anticipatory echoes is seen in Romans 4:19, which is about Abraham. There, Paul emphasizes that Abraham wasn't weak in faith. Could it be that Paul does this because he is concerned about those believers in Rome who *are* weak in faith and who are part of the debate that worries him? Notice these statements from Romans 14 and 15:

- Accept him whose faith is weak, without passing judgment on disputable matters (Romans 14:1).
- We who are strong ought to bear with the failings of the weak and not to please ourselves (Romans 15:1).

Paul uses the example of Abraham not only to buttress his theological arguments about grace and salvation for all, but also to undermine the disputes that make him worry about the unity of the Roman church.

Finally, Paul has spoken frequently about righteousness in all four of these beginning chapters. Then, in Romans 14, where Paul counsels the Romans about their disputes, he tells them that the kingdom of God isn't about food and drink—which is what they were arguing about. It's about righteousness (see verse 17). We will speak of this in more detail when we come to the final chapters.

Most of you who are reading this book are studying the book of Romans over the course of thirteen weeks. Remember that the Romans experienced it in one hour. The first chapters would still have been fresh in their minds when they came to the end; thus they would probably have noticed the connections between the theological message at the beginning of the letter and the practical, ethical concerns at its end. This should remind us that as we study Romans we are on a journey that is headed to a climax. That realization changes the way we read each part of the letter, including these early chapters.

CHAPTER 6

Expounding the Faith

So what?

In theology, that's always an important question. After all the theological jargon has been spoken, what difference does it make in actual life? In Romans 5, Paul stops for a "so what" moment. He's told us we are justified by faith. What difference does that make? We've been justified by faith—so what?

Paul was a pastor. He wasn't interested in theoretical musing for its own sake; he cared about everyday, practical life. That's why he began Romans 5 with the words, "Therefore, since we have been justified through faith . . ." What follows is a beautiful description of what it means to experience the gift of salvation he has just outlined. In other words, he answers the "so what."

He says that first of all, experiencing justification means having "peace with God through our Lord Jesus Christ" (Romans 5:1). Paul uses the word *peace* eleven times in Romans. In his day, this word was a broad one. More than the absence of war, it meant holistic well-being. To be at peace with God is to be in a right relationship with Him, being comfortable with Him, living without fear of Him. This, of course, is what righteousness is all about—*right relationships.*

Paul never even hints that God was at war with us. Remember, he sees even God's wrath as His turning away and giving us over to our own choices. His point is that we once lived in a state of rebellion against God, both fearing Him and feeling hostile toward Him. Now we live at peace with Him, knowing His gracious love for us.

Second, having been justified, we live our lives in a new atmosphere. In verse 2, Paul speaks of "gain[ing] access . . . [to the] grace in which we now stand." Grace—God's wonderful acceptance that we receive apart from anything we could do to earn it—becomes the atmosphere in which we live and breathe.

As I write these words, I'm in Southern California. For the past few weeks, we've been living in an atmosphere of smoke as fires burn around us. It's hardly the ideal atmosphere for the eyes or the lungs. We long for clear, clean air to breathe. Grace is the ideal clear, clean atmosphere for the spiritual life. When we breathe this atmosphere of grace, we live in joy and freedom. It's like standing in a whole new world.

The third practical result of the experience of justification is surprising. It's so surprising that many English translations, including the New International Version, hide it. The surprise is that those who are justified by faith *boast*! That's surprising because less than two chapters earlier, Paul said that faith excludes all boasting (Romans 3:27). Now he says that those who are justified by faith *boast*.

This seems so inconsistent that many translators substitute the word *rejoice* for the word *boast*. But *boast* is the best translation of the Greek word that Paul used. When he meant *rejoice*, he used a different Greek word. Paul purposely chose *boast* in this passage. If the word is translated "rejoice," then the reader loses the connection with Romans 3:27, and Paul used the same word in chapters 3 and 5 for a purpose. He didn't do it to be inconsistent but to emphasize the contrast between our old situation and this new atmosphere in which we live.

The kind of boasting that is excluded in chapter 3 is boasting that takes credit for our salvation or pats ourselves on the back for our goodness. The boasting that Paul allows—indeed, commends—in this chapter has an entirely different focus. It is boasting in God. It is such enthusiastic praise for God and what He has done for us that it allows us to boast even when from an earthly perspective things aren't going well. Paul uses the word three times in this chapter:

- Verse 2—We boast in the hope of God's glory.
- Verse 3—We boast in our sufferings.
- Verse 11—We boast in God.

Paul says that because we boast in God and in the confident hope that we will share in His glory, we can even boast in our suffering. Not that we enjoy suffering or would choose it, but we also "know that suffering produces perseverance; perseverance, character; and character, hope. And hope does not disappoint us" (Romans 5:3–5).

When Paul adds that hope doesn't disappoint us, the word translated "disappoint" in the original is stronger than the English translation suggests. Paul says that hope *doesn't put us to shame.* Paul lived in a world where shame and honor were important concepts. In our individualistic society, we tend to do our own thing without worrying about what others think. But in the more community-oriented world of the first century there was nothing worse than having the community look at you and see shame. It was almost as if shame were a mask worn on the face for all to see. Paul says that hope doesn't bring shame. Rather, it brings confidence. This turns the ordinary concept of shame and honor upside down. People in Paul's day thought that by boasting in their accomplishments they kept themselves from shame. Paul says that the only way we can avoid shame is by boasting in God and hoping in Him.

Peace with God, an atmosphere of grace, boasting in God whatever may happen, because we know that we live in hope—all these are the "so what" of the experience of justification by faith. But it gets even better. Paul goes on to summarize what God has done for us in Christ.

Through the Spirit, "God has poured out his love into our hearts" (verse 5). In the next three verses (6–8), Paul emphasizes that the measure of this love is Christ's death for us. His death came at just the right time. Paul had two words for "time" at his disposal, one that meant time in a merely chronological sense, and one that refers to a quality of time. He uses the second one here. It was the *opportune* time.

Christ's death also came at God's initiative, apart from anything we could have done. Paul uses three words in these three verses to emphasize our helplessness. He says that Christ died when we were "powerless," "ungodly," and "sinners." In other words, when we were in a mess and were too weak to do anything about it.

Paul intends this to be understood at both a cosmic and personal level. The world was sinful, and Christ died for the world and all its people. But He died for each of us too. And He died for us when we were powerless and sinful. This goes against the grain of normal human behavior. We won't die even for a righteous person, let alone a sinner. Well, Paul does say that we might die for a good person, probably meaning a winning, charismatic person (see verse 7). But the whole gospel is summed up well in Christ's uncharacteristic behavior: "While we were still sinners, Christ died for us" (verse 8).

Much more

In fifteenth-century Spain, a coin appeared that pictured the Pillars of Hercules, symbolizing the Strait of Gibraltar. An inscription on the coin read, "No more beyond." Thanks to Columbus and other explorers, the coin became obsolete. Around 1537, another coin appeared with the same picture but a new inscription: "Much more beyond." In Romans 5, Paul points to the "much more" that comes as a result of salvation by grace. He uses the expression four times. The first two times he uses the expression, he contrasts the present positive experience we have with the even greater promise of the future. In the second two, he contrasts the past negative legacy of Adam with the positive promise of our expectations in Christ. The following chart shows these contrasts:

Verse	Now	Future
9	Since we have now been justified by his [Christ's] blood,	how *much more* shall we be saved from God's wrath through him!
10	If, when we were God's enemies, we were reconciled to him through the death of his Son,	how *much more,* having been reconciled, shall we be saved through his life!
	Adam	**Christ**
15	If the many died by the trespass [sin] of the one man [Adam],	how *much more* did God's grace and the gift that came by the grace of the one man, Jesus Christ, overflow to the many!
17	If, by the trespass of the one man, death reigned through that one man,	how *much more* will those who receive God's abundant provision of grace and of the gift of righteousness reign in life through the one man, Jesus Christ.

The first two contrasts in verses 9 and 10 say something important about Paul's views of salvation and eschatology. For him, the second coming of Jesus is not just an event in the future that we hope will happen. It is already assured and guaranteed on the strength of what we have presently received from God. Our present experience of salvation is already the down payment on all that we hope for. If we have already been justified and are at peace with God, we know that He will save us eternally. If God loved us so much that He reconciled us to Himself through Christ when we were still enemies, how much more confident of salvation we can be now that we are friends. The present experience we enjoy assures our future hope.

Notice that it is God who is the subject—the One initiating the action—in this reconciliation. We did not reconcile ourselves to God. Nor did Christ do something to make God love us more and accept us. As is clear in verse 8, it is God who proved His love for us when Christ died for us sinners. God is the subject. He loves us from the beginning and acts in Christ to save us. Paul makes the same point in 2 Corinthians 5:19 when he says that "God was reconciling the world to himself in Christ."

There's an old heresy in the Christian church that is still very much in our bones. Somehow we tend to see God as the harsh and stern Father whom Jesus must beg to love us and not punish us. But that's not what Jesus' intercession means. Jesus doesn't have to change God's mind about us; God loves us from the beginning and is the One who is in Christ reconciling the world to Himself. Yet if you ask the children in a Sabbath School division to draw a picture of God the Father and another of Jesus, usually the pictures of Jesus will be much friendlier. Somehow we need to convey in all our teaching that God the Father loves us just as much as Jesus does.

This concept of reconciliation is yet another metaphor to add to the list we noted in chapter 4. The experience of salvation is not only like being acquitted by a judge, set free from slavery, or forgiven through a temple sacrifice; it is also like being reconciled to an enemy through the intercession of an ambassador.

Adam and Christ

In the culture of America, when we think of humanity, we begin with the autonomous human being. Humanity is made up of a collection of individuals. Individuals are the basic stuff of humanity. However, in biblical times, when people thought of humanity, they thought of a group or community. True, groups were made up of individuals, but the basic stuff of humanity was the community.

That difference stands behind the sustained analogy Paul begins in Romans 5:12.

Paul sees humans as being in community or solidarity with either Adam or Christ. We are naturally part of Adam's tribe or clan. We stand in a community of sinners characterized by Adam. But when we accept Christ, we enter a new community, one characterized by Christ. And there is a huge difference between these two communities.

Maybe we can understand this better if we think about our modern allegiance to sports teams. In baseball, I am a Dodgers fan. The youth pastor I work with is an Angels fan. When we go to a game between the Angels and the Dodgers, it isn't at all hard to tell the difference between us. Dodgers fans wear blue, and Angels fans wear red. We shout and cheer at different times. We are easily distinguishable.

Those who live in Adam and those who live in Christ are also easily distinguishable. Paul gives quite a list of the differences.

Verse	In Adam	In Christ
12, 15	Sin entered through him, and by his sin the many died.	Through Him, God's grace overflows.
16	He brings condemnation.	He brings justification.
17	Through him death reigned.	Through Him we reign in life.
18	He brings condemnation to all.	He brings life to all.
19	Through his disobedience the many were made sinners.	Through His obedience the many will be made righteous.

When Paul talks about "the many," he means all. All of us are either connected to Adam as sinners or to Christ as people of faith. Membership in one community means death; membership in the other means life. In Adam, death reigns and gets the best of all of us.

But in Christ, *we* actually reign and live in the atmosphere of God's grace with the assurance that our hope will not fail us. Paul has already shown us how we move from being in Adam to being in Christ: it is through faith.

Original sin

One of the persistent arguments over Romans 5 has revolved around the concept of original sin. Are we sinners because *we* sin or because we inherit *Adam's* sin? It isn't Paul's purpose to answer that question here; nevertheless, theologians have tried to use this chapter to answer the question. Much of the debate has centered on the translation of Romans 5:12. In the Greek in which Paul was composing this letter, the last phrase of this verse begins with a preposition and a pronoun that literally mean "in which" or "in whom." Since the time of Augustine, some have taken this to mean "in whom all sinned," the "whom" being Adam. Thus, they argue for an original sin passed on from Adam to all his posterity. We are all sinners because Adam sinned. We are born sinners because we receive sin as an inheritance from Adam.

Others, including almost all modern translators, take this preposition-pronoun combination to mean "because." With this reading, we are sinners not "in" Adam but "because" we sinned. Paul uses this particular preposition-pronoun structure in at least three other passages (2 Corinthians 5:4; Philippians 3:12; 4:12) and in each of those cases the meaning is "because." That's probably the way it should be translated here as well.

This does not, however, answer the question of how we become sinners. Are we born pure and then become sinners the first time we break the law? Or are we born sinners before the first time we break the law? Paul doesn't say; he simply puts us all in the category of sinners until we are grasped by God's grace and we put our trust in Him.

It doesn't take long for small children to reveal a certain pride, selfishness, or willfulness. If this isn't sin, it does tend to blossom into sin before long. I watched this in my youngest grandson this summer. We were on vacation with our daughter, son-in-law, and two grandsons on the Yucatán Peninsula in Mexico. It was a hot day. We had just visited the Mayan ruins in Tulum and had then walked down to the beach to cool off. My one-and-a-half-year-old grandson, Conlan, was hungry. He was also dirty and covered with sand. His dad got a granola bar, broke off a piece, and said, "Let me put this in your mouth. Your hands are too sandy for you to touch it." But when Conlan's dad tried to put the piece of bar in Conlan's mouth, Conlan issued a whole series of protests. It was obvious that he wanted to put it in his mouth himself. Eventually, his dad held him and put the bar in his mouth. But as soon as his dad was a few feet away, Conlan took the bar out of his mouth, held it up toward him in his dirty, sandy hands, and smiled big as if to say, "See, I won!" Then he put the bar in his mouth and ate it. We aren't very old before we think we have to come out on top. That attitude seems to be at the heart of who we are as humans. For Paul, that's what it means to be in Adam.

Paul believed that the sin problem began with Adam. That first man transgressed a specific command of God. The result of sin is death, and the fact that sin "reigned from the time of Adam to the time of Moses" (Romans 5:14) shows that sin was in the world even before God gave the law. When He gave the law, it revealed the nature and scope of sin. Even though sin was already in the world and was doing its damage, it wasn't plainly seen or understood until the law defined it. This is one way in which the law increased sin (see Romans 5:20).[1] But Paul concludes that when the law increased the sin that Adam had introduced, "grace increased all the more" (Romans 5:20). We don't have to live a sin-oriented life in solidarity with Adam. God's grace, available to *all* in Christ, far exceeds the problem of sin.

That raises the question, If grace can really cover any amount of sin, why shouldn't we go on sinning so that grace can increase all the more? There seems to be some kind of logic about that idea. Paul takes it up in Romans 6, as we will see in the next chapter.

---

1. It isn't the only way. Paul will show us another in Romans 7.

CHAPTER 7

Victory Over Sin

It is inevitable. Whoever teaches that we are saved by God's grace rather than by our works will be accused of being soft on sin. Paul was no exception. Remember Romans 3? There Paul acknowledged that his opponents were claiming that he taught it was all right to sin. They characterized his position this way: If God's grace takes care of our sin, we might as well live it up and sin as we please. If more sin equals more grace, then the more sin the better.

While Paul mentions this charge against him in chapter 3, he doesn't answer it there. He simply writes it off by saying that the condemnation of those who made those charges against him is just: "Someone might argue, 'If my falsehood enhances God's truthfulness and so increases his glory, why am I still condemned as a sinner?' Why not say—as we are being slanderously reported as saying and as some claim that we say—'Let us do evil that good may result'? Their condemnation is deserved" (Romans 3:7, 8).

The question, however, deserves an answer. After all, Paul did end chapter 5 by saying, "where sin increased, grace increased all the more" (Romans 5:20). Couldn't one legitimately conclude that we might as well keep on sinning? Let's keep that grace coming!

Paul answers this question in Romans 6. The entire chapter speaks to the basic question about sin and grace. But Paul asks the question in two ways and answers it with two different illustrations. Here are the two questions:

- Verse 1—Shall we go on sinning so that grace may increase?
- Verse 15—Shall we sin because we are not under law but under grace?

In both cases, Paul's answer is the same: "Absolutely not!"[1] This is a strong expression that could literally be translated, "Oh may it not be!" It's used fifteen times in the New Testament; all but once in Paul's letters.[2] Ten of the occurrences are in Romans (3:4, 6, 31; 6:2, 15; 7:7, 13; 9:14; 11:1, 11). Paul tends to use this expression when he's in a debate with imaginary opponents or objectors. He uses this strong negative to show clearly what he does *not* believe. He does *not* believe Christians should go on sinning because of grace.

Why does he not believe this? Two illustrations will make it clear.

The first illustration: Baptism

Paul uses baptism as his first illustration. He argues that if we really understand what happened when we were baptized, we couldn't take sin lightly. In baptism, we died to our old way of life—in other words, we died to sin—and we were resurrected to a new way of life. Baptism is death and burial with Christ, followed by resurrection with Him. If Christians have died to their old way of life, it makes no sense at all for them to go on living that old life. In verse 6, Paul calls this old way of life slavery to sin. He'll expound on that much more in the second half of the chapter, but it is apparent here that sin is a power that enslaves the sinner.

In verse 12, Paul uses another analogy that gives the same idea. He tells Christians not to "let sin reign" over them. Here the image is of a king ruling his subjects. In either case—whether sin enslaves us as a master or rules over us as a king—it's clear that Paul believes sin to be more than just a matter of isolated, individual decisions to break God's law.

Victory Over Sin

When we think of a biblical definition of sin, we usually think of 1 John 3:4, "sin is the transgression of the law" (KJV). That might lead us to believe that sin is simply the occasional bad decision one makes to break the law. For Paul, however, sin is much more than that. It's a power that controls us and keeps us from having a positive relationship with God. It forces us onto a path that inevitably leads to death. It is a destructive force that we can't overcome. As we will see when we study Romans 7, this power is closely tied to the law. We will see that sin takes advantage of the law to increase its hold on us. Solving the sin problem is not merely a matter of deciding to make better decisions. Rather, it's a matter of breaking free from the control of a force that compels us to live in a way that leads to death.

In that sense, sin is always destructive. It destroys relationships and life itself. Everything that God forbids in the law is destructive. But when the destructive force of sin has control of us, we can't escape on our own. The only way we can escape from the old life of sin is to die. We need more than just a spiritual tune-up—we need death.

And that is what baptism symbolizes—death to this force of sin that controls us and leads us to destruction. Therefore, Paul says, "We know that our old self was crucified with him so that the body of sin might be done away with, that we should no longer be slaves to sin—because anyone who has died has been freed from sin" (Romans 6:6, 7).

Notice that in this place Paul is using baptism as an illustration. His subject isn't baptism; it's whether or not we should go on sinning because of God's grace. Baptism illustrates *why* we shouldn't go on sinning. Our baptism was our acceptance of Jesus' death and resurrection for us. In it we died and were buried with Him. That old way of life in which the power of sin controlled us is gone. Now we have arisen to a new life of freedom from the power of sin. In the light of this good news, Paul gives us several admonitions in verses 11–14:

- Count yourselves dead to sin.
- Count yourselves . . . alive to God.
- Do not let sin reign in your mortal body.
- Do not offer the parts of your body to sin, as instruments of wickedness.
- Offer yourselves to God.
- Offer the parts of your body to [God] as instruments of righteousness.

These admonitions all assume the good news of God's grace. Believers can obey them because they've already died to sin. This leads, then, to the conclusion that Paul reaches at the end of the first part of the chapter: "Sin shall not be your master, because you are not under law, but under grace" (verse 14).

So being under grace rather than under the law doesn't mean sinning as we please. Quite the opposite. It means that sin is no longer our master. In the new atmosphere of grace in which we live, we are freed from the destructive force of sin that kept us from having peace with God and from living in harmony with our brothers and sisters. This doesn't mean that Christians are sinless and never make mistakes. But it does mean that the destructive force of sin is no longer our master.

Even though baptism is an illustration and not the subject of this first half of Romans 6, we do learn about baptism from the way Paul uses this illustration. If baptism is a symbol of the believer's burial and resurrection with Christ, then immersion—in which the person being baptized actually goes down into the water and is covered by it—is the only appropriate symbol of this experience. It's also clear from what Paul says that baptism is a symbol of the believer's decision to identify with Christ's death and resurrection and to choose solidarity with Christ. And since baptism represents a decision or a choice, then those who participate in it must be of sufficient age and maturity to make thoughtful decisions.

In baptism, we identify with Christ so fully that in a real sense it was not only Christ who died on the cross two thousand years ago—

we also died with Him. The people that we were, dominated by sin, no longer live. In baptism we also unite ourselves with the hope of the resurrection, so that even though we live in a world of sin and death, we already live in the confidence of the end. This is why we can consider ourselves dead to sin and be confident that because Christ died for sin once and for all (verse 10) and was raised, never to die again (verse 9), we can be certain that we will live with Him. This picture of union with Christ, symbolized in baptism, is perhaps the richest source of material for theological reflection on the meaning of baptism to be found anywhere in the New Testament.

The second illustration: Slavery

In the second half of Romans 6, Paul expounds on an issue he raised in the first half: slavery. First, he re-asks the question in different words: "Shall we sin because we are not under law but under grace?" (verse 15). Again his strong answer is, Absolutely not! This time the reason is that to go on sinning is to be a slave of sin. For Paul, we are all slaves. We are either slaves of sin or we are slaves of God. He doesn't even consider the possibility of our not being slaves at all. Ultimately, there are only two choices—pick your slavery.

Such a notion would have seemed less surprising in Paul's day than it does today, since it's estimated that slaves made up one-third of the population of Rome. Slavery was a common part of everyday life. It's likely that some of the members of the church in Rome were slaves. At the end of this letter, when Paul greets "those in the household of Narcissus" (Romans 16:11), he is probably referring to slaves. And there were apparently slaves with Paul in Corinth as he wrote this letter. Tertius, the scribe who wrote the letter as Paul dictated it (verse 22), and Quartus, who sends greetings to the church (verse 23), were probably both slaves since their names meant "third" and "fourth," as I noted earlier, a common way of naming slaves.

In Paul's day, the treatment of slaves varied from one end of the spectrum to the other. Some slaves were trusted stewards and tutors, while others were kept in the most degrading conditions. The following

excerpts from the moral letters of one of the Roman philosophers—
Seneca, the brother of Gallio, the proconsul at Corinth before whom
Paul once appeared (see Acts 18:12–17)—show that philosophers
argued that slaves should be treated with respect, but also demon-
strate how slaves were often mistreated by the rich who lived in
wanton luxury:

> I am glad to learn, through those who come from you,
> that you live on friendly terms with your slaves. This befits a
> sensible and well-educated man like yourself. "They are
> slaves," people declare. Nay, rather they are men. "Slaves!"
> No, comrades. "Slaves!" No, they are unpretentious friends.
> "Slaves!" No, they are our fellow-slaves, if one reflects that
> Fortune has equal rights over slaves and free men alike.[3]

> When we recline at a banquet, one slave mops up the dis-
> gorged food, another crouches beneath the table and gathers
> up the left-overs of the tipsy guests. Another carves the price-
> less game birds; with unerring strokes and skilled hand he
> cuts choice morsels along the breast or the rump. Hapless fel-
> low, to live only for the purpose of cutting fat capons cor-
> rectly, unless, indeed, the other man is still more unhappy
> than he, who teaches this art for pleasure's sake, rather than
> he who learns it because he must. Another, who serves the
> wine, must dress like a woman and wrestle with his advanc-
> ing years; he cannot get away from his boyhood; he is dragged
> back to it; and though he has already acquired a soldier's fig-
> ure, he is kept beardless by having his hair smoothed away or
> plucked out by the roots, and he must remain awake through-
> out the night, dividing his time between his master's drunk-
> enness and his lust; in the chamber he must be a man, at the
> feast a boy. . . .With slaves like these the master cannot bear
> to dine; he would think it beneath his dignity to associate
> with his slave at the same table! Heaven forfend![4]

Even though Paul's readers were familiar with slavery, no one wanted to be a slave. But Paul says that we are all slaves and we must pick our slavery. The slaveries we have to choose between are incredibly different. The first, slavery to sin, "leads to death" (Romans 6:16). That is what sin is all about. It is destructive. It destroys life. For Paul, "the wages of sin is death" (verse 23). The word Paul uses that's translated "wages" here is a term that referred originally to the most meager wages earned for the most difficult work. It meant the rations that soldiers were given when at war. The common soldier's pay has never been extravagant, and what harder work can one imagine? So in the first kind of slavery, one works hard only to earn death.

The other slavery couldn't be more different. In it, the free "gift of God is eternal life" (verse 23). Paul had several words at his disposal for wages and gifts. The word he uses here is for the freest of gifts. It is from the same root as is the Greek word *grace* that is so important in this letter. What you get in return for serving God as a slave is an absolutely free gift that turns out to be eternal life. What a contrast! How could anyone want to go on being a slave of sin?

And Paul says that when we're under grace, we're not living a life of sin. Emphasizing grace is not being soft on sin. Being under grace means being free from the destructive force of sin that leads us to death.

A nineteenth-century would-be poet wrote, "Free from the law— O happy condition! I can sin as I please, and still have remission." That poet had it all wrong. If we understand the true nature of sin and its destructive force, being in sin could hardly have any appeal.

A contemporary illustration

Maybe we can use a contemporary illustration to help capture what Paul is saying here. Suppose two people get married. They are thoroughly in love and have a wonderful marriage. But after some time the husband seems to be growing more distant; the wife notices that he is less attentive, forgets important occasions, and is gone more and more often.

Finally, she learns the terrible truth: her husband is having an affair. And not only is he having an affair, he is having the affair with her best friend. The wife is devastated. She's been betrayed by the two best friends she's had. How could she ever forgive them?

At first, she feels that she can't, that she must end the marriage. For a time she and her husband separate. But she really does love him. So, after a deeply painful struggle, she asks her husband if he's willing to renew his vows of love to her and to reestablish their home. It isn't easy. The hurt has gone deep. But when he responds positively, she promises that she will, to the very best of her ability, forgive completely and act as if the affair never happened. And so they move back in together.

Suppose the husband now said, "This is great! I know that my wife will forgive me, so I can go out and have all the affairs I want and continue to be forgiven. Am I ever going to live it up now!" You'd probably say, "This guy just doesn't get it. His wife's willingness to forgive didn't come easily. The hurt he caused went deep. The affair was destructive to the relationship. Why would he want to cause such pain and destruction again?"

This is much the situation we're in. We've been slaves to a destructive force within us that Paul calls "sin." God paid dearly for our forgiveness and our new standing with Him. He gave His Son for us. For us to say that we might as well go on sinning because God is gracious totally misunderstands both the destructive nature of sin and what it cost God to offer us His grace so freely. Shall we continue to sin because we are under grace? Absolutely not!

---

1. As noted in a previous chapter, this is the author's translation of Paul's expression.—Ed.

2. For the other use, see Luke 20:16.

3. Seneca, *Ad Lucilium Epistulae Morales,* vol. 1, ed. G. P. Goold, trans. Richard M. Gummere, Loeb Classical Library (Cambridge, Mass.: Harvard University Press, 1979), 301–303.

4. Ibid., 305.

CHAPTER 8

The Law and the Man of Romans 7

Have you ever heard a sermon that included a powerful illustration within it—a story so powerful that long after you forgot what the sermon was about and maybe even who preached it, you still remembered the story? Stories and illustrations have the power to stay in our memories like nothing else.

Paul was a preacher, and a good one. Like all good preachers, he used illustrations. In Romans 6, he used two of them: baptism and slavery. His topic wasn't either baptism or slavery. Rather, it was the question of whether Christians under grace should continue to sin. But he used baptism and slavery to illustrate his answer, which was "Absolutely not!"

In Romans 7, Paul moves to a new topic—the law—and he uses not two but three illustrations to make his point. But the illustrations have proven to be so interesting that many commentators have focused their attention on them rather than on the point Paul was making. In fact, the illustrations are so compelling in themselves that it is easy to forget what the chapter is actually about. It is about the law, and the three illustrations are marriage, the tenth commandment, and the personal struggle of one who wants to do right but ends up doing wrong. As we consider these illustrations, it's important that we keep our focus on the subject at hand—the law—

and that we watch for what each illustration teaches about the law.

Why does Paul need to talk about the law at this point? Someone who has read the letter to the Romans thus far could hardly be blamed for being a bit confused about the law. Paul has told us that we are saved "apart from [the] law" (Romans 3:21). But he's also said that we don't abolish the law through faith; rather, we strengthen it (verse 31). He's just spent a chapter showing that we are no longer under the law, but then he has also said that this doesn't mean we can sin and violate the law. So how are we to put all of this together?

At first, we might find what Paul has to say about the law in this chapter a bit confusing too. On the one hand, the law seems to be a menacing culprit. Look what it does.

- It arouses sinful passions (Romans 7:5).
- It reveals sin (verse 7).
- It serves as an impetus to sin (verse 8).
- It even brings death (verse 10).

All this makes it sound like everything would be all right if we could just get rid of that miserable law. But on the other hand, Paul can also say of the law:

- It is holy, righteous, and good (verse 12).
- It is spiritual (verse 14).

Paul's three illustrations will help us see how the law can be dangerous and good, threatening and necessary, all at the same time. In its own way, each of the illustrations will show that Paul's problem with the law is not with the *content* of the law. His problem is with the *misuse* of the law. People misuse the law in two primary ways. They attempt to rely on the law, rather than on God, for salvation. They also view the law in a way that divides people and excludes some of them from the sphere of God's grace.

The marriage illustration (Romans 7:1-6)

Paul says we all know that when a woman marries a man, she is bound to that man by the law of marriage as long as they both live. For her to live with another man when her husband is alive would be to commit adultery. But if her husband dies, the whole situation changes. Then she is free to marry any man she chooses. Death brings an end to the obligations of the law of marriage.

So what does that obvious fact have to do with the law? Paul said in Romans 6:11 that as Christians, we have died to sin. Now he adds that we have died to the law. We were married to the law, but now we have died to it and are free to marry another. We are free to marry Christ and to live with Him. Thus, Paul is contrasting two ways of life. In one we are married to the law; in the other we die to the law and live in the Spirit with Christ. In one we live according to the "flesh"; in the other we live according to the Spirit.

What's the difference between these two ways of life? In the first we bore fruit for death. Why? Because we were living according to the flesh. Paul uses this term twenty-three times in Romans—three times in this chapter and ten times in Romans 8. The New International Version usually translates the Greek original by the expression "sinful nature." For Paul, flesh isn't simply material or bodily existence, nor is it an identifiable part of the whole human being. Rather, it's the whole human person subject to the law of sin and death. With this term Paul points to humans in their mortality and their tendency to respond to sin. The life of slavery to sin is life in the flesh. What's more, in this way of life, the law is an external written code. In other words, I keep the law because I have to. The law says, "Don't steal," so I don't steal. The law is something that stands outside me and orders me to live in a certain way.

For Paul, not stealing is a good thing. But when the law is simply an external code, we have no power to overcome the desire to steal. Not wanting to steal is an even better thing than not stealing. When we live the new life of being married to Christ and living by the Spirit rather than by the written code, we have new power and new direction in our lives. We come into harmony with the law; and we bear fruit to God. Notice this summary of the difference between the two ways of life as given in Romans 7:5, 6.

The Old Way	In Christ
We're married to the law.	We're married to Christ.
We're controlled by the flesh.	We're controlled by the Spirit.
The law is an external, written code.	The law is internal because of the Spirit.
We bear fruit to death.	We bear fruit to God.

Notice that the difference between these two ways is not that one includes the law and the other excludes it. The difference is in the role the law plays and where it is in relationship to our lives. In the old way, we look to the law to save us, but it can't. We may try to keep it, but we end up failing because we are controlled by the flesh, and the law can't overpower that control. In the new way, Christ saves us. He *does* have power to break the control of the flesh. He sends His Spirit to live in our lives, and the law is internalized in us, for the Spirit that lives in us guides us according to the values of the law.

So the first illustration about the law shows us that the problem is not with the law but with the role that the law plays in our lives.

The tenth-commandment illustration (Romans 7:7-13)

The second illustration reveals the same basic point and in a way that may be easier to understand. In the first illustration, Paul puts sin and the law so close together that we might get the idea that they are the same. So Paul asks, "Is the law sin?" (verse 7). His answer is another "Absolutely not!" The law reveals sin. But it does even more. It also helps produce sin—or at least serves as a catalyst for sin.

To show what he means, Paul turns to the tenth commandment: " 'You shall not covet' " (Exodus 20:17). He says he "would not have known what coveting really was" all about if the law hadn't told him not to do it (Romans 7:7). So the law revealed his covetousness. But it did more. When the law said, "Don't covet," Paul's natural reaction was to covet. So the law actually stirred up coveting.

When my son was a small boy (he's now grown and has his own son), we used to play a game. I would say to him, "Larry, I'm going to count to ten and I don't want you to laugh while I'm counting." At that point he'd get a very resolute look on his face and determine not to laugh before I got to ten. Then I'd start counting, "One, two . . ." By the time I reached three, the resolute look was turning into a smile, and by the time I got to about five, he was laughing so hard he could hardly stand up. Now, when we weren't playing the game, he could easily go ten seconds without laughing. But when I focused his attention on not laughing, he was absolutely powerless to refrain from laughing.

That is how Paul sees the tenth commandment. When the law says, "Don't covet," he finds himself coveting all the more. The law puts the idea of coveting in his mind, and once it is there, he can't help himself. It's as if I told you not to think about a blue dog. What do you immediately think about? Once I put the idea in your mind, you can't help yourself.

Now, the tenth commandment works especially well for this illustration, since it deals with motives, not just actions. It's one thing not to steal, but it's much more difficult to keep from wanting things that belong to another person. Of course, one could draw the conclusion from this that the law is terrible because it stirs up sin. But again, Paul has no problem with the *content* of the law. He can say that "the law is holy, and the commandment is holy, righteous and good" (Romans 7:12). The problem isn't with the law. The problem is with sin, which Paul sees as a power that controls. And it doesn't just cause us to make the occasional bad decision. It is, as we saw in Romans 6, a power that enslaves and leads to death. Sin is so powerful that it can use the law to its own advantage. It seizes on the law and produces even more sin.

But what sin does with the law isn't the law's fault! The final of the three illustrations makes this point even more clearly, and it shows us whose fault it really is.

The human-dilemma illustration (Romans 7:14-25)

In this illustration, Paul points poignantly to the human dilemma that we've all felt. We find ourselves doing what we don't want to do and not doing what we want to do. Is there anyone who can't identify with the following words, which are selected from Romans 7:15–24?

> I do not understand what I do. For what I want to do I do not do, but what I hate I do. . . . For I have the desire to do what is good, but I cannot carry it out. For what I do is not the good I want to do; no, the evil I do not want to do—this I keep on doing. . . .
>
> So I find this law at work: When I want to do good, evil is right there with me. For in my inner being I delight in God's law; but I see another law at work in the members of my body, waging war against the law of my mind and making me a prisoner of the law of sin at work within my members. What a wretched man I am! Who will rescue me from this body of death?

Who is the "I" who speaks in this powerful passage? Commentators have made many suggestions. Some see Paul's words as autobiographical, but then they argue as to which period of his life these words come from. Others see the "I" as a type or symbol, but they disagree about what it represents. Some see the passage as an example of the Christian life as we grow and want to improve but find ourselves growing at a much slower rate than we want. Others say such a focus on "I" couldn't come from a Christian, but rather represents the pre-Christian life. Yet others are more specific and see the "I" as a person who has come to conviction about the law, but hasn't yet found Christ and is trying to live the Christian life on their own.

Is there any way of knowing who Paul is actually talking about?

It may well be that if Paul were to hear all these positions, he would simply laugh and say, "You missed my point." Paul isn't trying to talk about the human dilemma at some point in a person's experience. He's talking about the law, and the human dilemma is merely an illustration. You can see this in Romans 7:20, where Paul says, "Now if I do what I do not want to do, it is no longer I who do it, but it is sin living in me that does it."

Here's what Paul is trying to get across. There's a gap between what we want to do and what we actually do; what we want to be and what we actually are. It's likely that we experience this gap to some degree at every stage of life. The very existence of this gap shows that the problem is not the law, for in wanting to be a better person and to live according to the law, I affirm its *content*. The problem is not with the law but with the sinful nature—what Paul calls the "flesh"—which keeps me from doing what I want to do. Remember, the topic is not the human dilemma; it's the law. The fact that there is a human dilemma—that we don't live up to our own ideals—shows that *we* have a problem. The problem isn't the law—it's us!

So Paul's answer is not to get rid of the law. Nor is it to sin and violate the law. The answer must be something that comes from outside of ourselves and is more powerful than the sin that lives in us and continually pulls us off course. The answer, therefore, can only be God's grace, which comes from outside of ourselves to break the power of sin and death. Paul declares this answer at the end of chapter 7. He says, "Who will rescue me from this body of death? Thanks be to God—through Jesus Christ our Lord!" (verses 24, 25). Although he declares the answer here, he doesn't explain it until we come to Romans 8. There he outlines the difference between life in the flesh and life in the Spirit.

All three of Paul's illustrations in this chapter make the same point: sin poses a problem that we can't overcome. The law doesn't solve the problem. It can't save; it was never intended to save. In fact, it can actually make the sin problem worse. Only

God's gracious intervention through Jesus Christ can solve the problem. Only He can save. But this doesn't mean that the law is bad or should be ignored.

In this regard Paul is quite different from his Jewish colleagues of the day. Although the *Mishnah,* the codified teaching of the rabbis, wasn't written down for about one hundred fifty years after Paul's time, it represents a long history of oral tradition. In the *Mishnah,* the rabbis taught that God had created an evil inclination in humans called the evil *yetzer.* This evil *yetzer* had some similarities with what we would call "ego" and therefore served a good purpose in motivating people. But it also tempted them to evil. The law was the antidote that held the evil *yetzer* in check. In one passage, God, according to the rabbis, says, " 'I created within you the evil *yetzer,* but I created the Law as a drug. As long as you occupy yourselves with the Law, the *yetzer* will not rule over you. But if you do not occupy yourselves with the Torah, then you will be delivered into the power of the *yetzer,* and all its activity will be against you.' "[1]

For these rabbis, the law was the solution to the problem of the evil *yetzer* that lives in human beings. For Paul, the power of sin is much more pervasive and persistent than the *yetzer.* As holy and just and good as the law is, concentrating on it won't get rid of the problem. Only Christ can do that. In the next chapter, we'll see how.

---

1. Kiddushin 30b, quoted in C. K. Barrett, ed., *The New Testament Background: Selected Documents* (New York: Harper and Row, 1961), 153.

CHAPTER 9

The Promise of Freedom in Christ

"Promises, promises!" The very way we say those words is evidence of our cynicism about promises. And we have good reason for cynicism. From political speeches to television commercials, we constantly hear promises that we know aren't believable. I'm reminded of a cartoon I saw once. When a new president is elected and comes to the White House, a transition team helps get things ready for the new administration. The cartoon defined the transition team as the group that transforms campaign pledges into broken promises.

Romans 8 is a chapter full of promises. Incredible promises, but trustworthy promises. If Romans 7 captures the frustration of the cycle of sin, guilt, and death, Romans 8 is overwhelming in its presentation of the promise of victory, freedom, life, and hope. Let's examine these promises one by one.

The promise of no condemnation

Paul begins Romans 8 by saying, "There is now no condemnation for those who are in Christ Jesus, because through Christ Jesus the law of the Spirit of life set me free from the law of sin and death" (verses 1, 2). Here the term *law* is used in the sense of "system" or "method." Paul is contrasting two different systems of living. One is slavery to the law of sin and death. In the previous two chapters, we have seen the shape of this system. Now Paul sets out a contrasting system—that of freedom through the Spirit of life. In this system there is no condemnation. Romans 8 will show us the shape of this new, free system of life through a series of promises. By the time we have surveyed the promises, we will understand why there is no condemnation for those in Christ Jesus.

This promise is "for those who are in Christ Jesus." For Paul this means becoming part of Christ's body—part of His new community that embraces both Jew and Gentile. Remember, Paul's concern is not simply individual salvation. Justification isn't simply the release of an individual from guilt. It is God's way of setting everything right. The problem that needs fixing is not just individual sin, but exclusiveness and alienation among people and between humans and God. God wants to create a new community in which all people, both Jew and Gentile, will come together in fellowship with Him.

All this is made possible because God sends His Spirit. Here Paul probably has Ezekiel in the back of his mind. Ezekiel wrote, " ' "This is what the Sovereign LORD says: . . . I will give you a new heart and put a new spirit in you; I will remove from you your heart of stone and give you a heart of flesh. And I will put my Spirit in you and move you to follow my decrees and be careful to keep my laws. You will live in the land I gave your forefathers; you will be my people, and I will be your God" ' " (36:22, 26–28). Paul carries the great promise of Ezekiel even further.

This leads us to the next promise, the promise of God's Spirit.

The promise of life in the Spirit

The basic difference in this second system of life is the indwelling Spirit of God. What the law could not do—save us and free us from death—Christ has done and continues to do by sending His Spirit to live in and among us. Paul says that the just requirements of the law are fulfilled in us when we live according to the Spirit rather than the flesh (Romans 8:4). This doesn't mean that Christians are sinless, but that the true requirements of the law—a trust in God and a life focused on Him—result from the Spirit living in us.

In order to understand this promise, we have to understand the sustained and significant contrast between the words *flesh* and *Spirit* in the first part of this chapter. It is hard to see this contrast because modern translations use so many different terms, such as "carnal" and "sinful nature," to translate the Greek term Paul used that literally means "flesh." As we noticed in the last chapter, by the term *flesh* Paul doesn't mean the physical body but that part of human life that is self-centered and is controlled by the power of sin.

Paul used the term *flesh* thirteen times in verses 3 through 13. Look at the following chart and notice what he says about the flesh. It should give you a good idea of what it means to live life in the "flesh." Notice that only the New Revised Standard Version makes the frequency of Paul's usage clearly visible by consistently translating the Greek word *sarx* by the same English word, *flesh*.

The Term *Flesh* in Romans 8:3–13			
Verse	What Paul Says	King James Translation	New International Version	New Revised Standard Version
3	The law was weakened by the flesh	Flesh	Sinful nature	Flesh
3	God sent His Son in the likeness of sinful flesh	Flesh	Sinful man	Flesh
3	Christ condemned sin in the flesh	Flesh	Sinful man	Flesh
4	In Christ we do not walk after the flesh	Flesh	Sinful nature	Flesh
5	Those of the flesh—	Flesh	[Sinful] nature	Flesh

5	Do the things of the flesh	Carnally	Sinful man	Flesh
6	To have the mind-set of the flesh is death	Carnal	Sinful mind	Flesh
7	The flesh mind is hostile to God	Flesh	Sinful nature	Flesh
8	Those in the flesh cannot please God	Flesh	Sinful nature	Flesh
9	You are not in the flesh	Flesh	Sinful nature	Flesh
12	You are not debtors to the flesh—	Flesh	Sinful nature	Flesh
12	To live according to the flesh	Flesh	It	Flesh
13	If you live after the flesh, you will die	Flesh	Sinful nature	Flesh

Clearly, to live the life of the flesh is bad. That life is hostile to God, dependent on self, and headed for death. But according to Paul, no one has to live the life of the flesh because God has defeated that way of life by sending Christ to live in the likeness of sinful flesh. Now Christ sends His Spirit to live in all who open their lives to Him. And what a contrast! Life in the Spirit is the opposite of life in the flesh.

In the following table we see that in verses 2 to 14, Paul uses the term *Spirit* thirteen times. Notice the difference this life produces.

The Term *Spirit* in Romans 8:2–14	
Verse	**What Paul Says**
2	The law of the Spirit of life sets us free.

4	We live according to the Spirit.
5	Those who live according to the Spirit . . .
5	have their minds set on what the Spirit desires.
6	The mind-set of the Spirit is life.
9	You are controlled by the Spirit, . . .
9	If you do not have the Spirit, you do not belong to Christ.
10	The Spirit is life.
11	The Spirit of Him who raised Jesus from the dead enlivens you . . .
11	by the Spirit that dwells in you.
13	If by the Spirit you put to death the misdeeds of the body, you will live.
14	Those led by the Spirit are children of God.

The Christian life is possible only because God sends His Spirit to live in the Christian to guide and direct a new and different kind of life, a life of freedom and of hope. This is one of the great promises that enable Christians to live without condemnation.

The promise of adoption as God's children

Paul says that the Spirit also makes us God's children and His heirs: "You did not receive a spirit of slavery to fall back into fear, but you have received a spirit of adoption. When we cry, 'Abba! Father!' it is that very Spirit bearing witness with our spirit that we are children of God, and if children, then heirs, heirs of God and joint heirs with Christ—if, in fact, we suffer with him so that we may also be glorified with him" (Romans 8:15–17, NRSV).

This is yet another of the many metaphors Paul uses in Romans to show what God has done for us in Christ. We are adopted as God's very own children. In fact, we have the privilege of calling Him *Abba*. This was an Aramaic term for "father"—the familiar term used by little children for their fathers. All parents are anxious for their children to recognize them and to call them by name, so almost all languages use simple sounds that children naturally make for those first names for parents—words like *Dada* and *Papa. Abba* is another such word. Ordinarily, this word wasn't used for addressing God. But according to Mark 14:35, 36, Jesus used it at the crucial moment in the Garden the night before He died. "Going a little farther, he fell to the ground and prayed that if possible the hour might pass from him. ' "Abba, Father," ' he said, ' "everything is possible for you. Take this cup from me. Yet not what I will, but what you will." ' "

Paul says that now we have the privilege of addressing God in the same, familiar way, for He has adopted us, taken us into His house, and made us His heirs. Obviously, we have no condemnation if we are His own children adopted into His family.

There is a striking contrast to this promise in rabbinic literature:

Why is the Exodus from Egypt mentioned in connection with every single commandment? The matter can be compared to a king, the son of whose friend was taken prisoner. The king ransomed him, not as son, but as slave, so that, if at any time he should disobey the king, the latter could say, "You are my slave." So, when he came back, the king said, "Put on my sandals for me, take my clothes to the bath house." Then the man protested. The king took out the bill of sale, and said, "You are my slave." So when God redeemed the children of Abraham his friend, he redeemed them, not as children, but as slaves, so that if he imposed upon them decrees, and they obeyed not, he could say, "Ye are my slaves."[1]

In contrast to this statement, Paul specifically says we are not slaves, but children. And if we are adopted into God's own family, not only does the promise have implications for our individual salvation, but it also speaks to the new reality that we are part of God's family, united together as Jew and Gentile in Christ.

The promise of a future better than earthly suffering

In Romans 8:18, Paul says, "I consider that our present sufferings are not worth comparing with the glory that will be revealed in us." He goes on to emphasize that it is not only humans, but the whole creation that groans in suffering while waiting for God to bring about His ultimate revelation. At the moment, our adoption and inheritance are ours in hope, but we have the assurance that eventually, they'll be ours in reality. When that time comes, we'll consider our suffering insignificant in comparison with what we receive. This is not at all to diminish the horror of this world's suffering. No one can read the newspaper on any given day and fail to recoil at the evil in this world and the horrendous suffering it causes. But the glory to be revealed is so much greater that it outweighs even this suffering.

At this point, however, we must rest in hope. We don't yet see the final glory, which Paul calls "the redemption of our bodies" (verse 23), but what we do already have gives us the assurance that we can wait patiently (verse 25).[2] The final salvation comes when our bodies are transformed or resurrected at the last day. Paul knows nothing of bodiless existence. The final hope is not that we'll escape our bodies but that God will redeem our bodies so that they'll lose their mortality. Simultaneous with this redemption is the end of decay and death in creation as well. We're part of creation, and our redemption requires the complete end of death.

By tying Christians with creation in this way, Paul shows us our solidarity with the environment in which we live. Both it and we are God's creation. This should give Christians a special sense of care for the environment. We are doubly tied to it—by both creation and redemption. God cares for the creation and will redeem it with us.

If He cares for creation, how can we do less?

The promise of assistance in our prayers

According to Paul, we don't even know how to pray, but the Spirit also helps us here. The Spirit translates our prayers into the prayers that we would pray if we really knew what was best for ourselves. In verses 26, 27, Paul says, "We do not know what we ought to pray for, but the Spirit himself intercedes for us with groans that words cannot express. And he who searches our hearts knows the mind of the Spirit, because the Spirit intercedes for the saints in accordance with God's will."

We need to remember that the Spirit's intercession for us isn't a matter of His trying to get God to change His mind about us and do something for us that He might not otherwise do. The Spirit who dwells in us is God's own Spirit. God's attitude toward us is no different than that of His Spirit. It is because God is our *Abba* that He dwells in us through His Spirit. And as a good parent, He doesn't merely give us what we ask for, He responds to our needs, including those we're not aware of.

I once heard a rabbi tell an old Jewish story about prayer. A man had left God, gone the way of the world, and quit coming to worship. One night when he was out living it up and getting drunk, he remembered that the next day was the Day of Atonement, the holiest and most important day of the Jewish calendar. He realized how far he had fallen and decided to repent. When he awoke in the morning with a terrible hangover, he remembered his desire to repent and decided to pray the prayers of repentance for the Day of Atonement. Unlike most of the prayers in our churches, which are spontaneous, these were written, liturgical prayers that were memorized and repeated. But this man, with his hangover, tried and tried but couldn't remember the prayers. Finally, he turned to God and said, "Lord, You know how sorry I am. I want to return to You, but I can't remember the prayers. In fact, the only thing I can remember is the alphabet. I will recite the alphabet. Please take the letters and put them together into the right prayers." The rabbi said that this man's prayer pleased God more than any other. I think this story fits with Paul's point here.

The promise that God works for our good

In verse 28, Paul says that in everything "God works for the good of those who love him." He has predestined them for salvation.[3] This doesn't mean that God causes evil. But when evil happens, God is there working for good. He's the kind of God who is constantly turning tragedies into triumphs.

The promise that we are "super winners"

The promises in this chapter just get better and better. Paul now says,

What, then, shall we say in response to this? If God is for us, who can be against us? He who did not spare his own Son, but gave him up for us all—how will he not also, along with him, graciously give us all things? Who will bring any charge against those whom God has chosen? It is God who justifies. Who is he that condemns? Christ Jesus, who died—more than that, who was raised to life—is at the right hand of God and is also interceding for us. Who shall separate us from the love of Christ? Shall trouble or hardship or persecution or famine or nakedness or danger or sword? As it is written:

"For your sake we face death all day long;
   we are considered as sheep to be slaughtered."

No, in all these things we are more than conquerors through him who loved us (verses 31–38).

Paul seems to have had an Old Testament text in mind when he wrote these words—Isaiah 50:7–9, which reads,

Because the Sovereign LORD helps me,

I will not be disgraced.
Therefore have I set my face like flint,
 and I know I will not be put to shame.
He who vindicates me is near.
 Who then will bring charges against me?
 Let us face each other!
Who is my accuser?
 Let him confront me!
It is the Sovereign LORD who helps me.
 Who is he that will condemn me?

The point is that if God is on your side, it really doesn't matter who is against you. And we know that God is on our side because He handed Jesus over for us (Romans 8:32).[4]

Paul takes up Isaiah's point to affirm that God is with us and is for us. Who then can be against us? Who can charge us? Who can condemn us? Would Christ condemn us? Of course not. He is the One who died for us and is at God's right hand, interceding for us. All this means is that there is absolutely nothing that could separate us from Christ's love. Not "trouble or hardship or persecution or famine or nakedness or danger or sword." That is quite a list. But in verse 37, Paul goes on to say that even "in all these things we are more than conquerors."

When Paul says we are "more than conquerors"—or, in other words, winners—he uses a word that appears only once in the New Testament. It is the combination of two Greek words, the word for victory, *nikoo*, the verb form of *nikē*, and the word *hyper*, which means "over," "beyond," or "more than." The latter word is the equivalent of our word *hyper*. Paul is saying that we are hyperwinners or super winners, not because we are stronger or faster than anybody else, but because Christ is more powerful than anything Satan can throw at us, even death itself.

This word *nikē*—"victory"—has an interesting background. Along with the great temples like the Parthenon, a little temple dedicated to the goddess *Nike*, the goddess of victory, stands on the

Acropolis in Athens. Paul once preached in the shadow of this temple (see Acts 17). It was to this goddess that the Greeks turned for victory, usually in sporting events and war.

Nike has become a proper name in English in precisely the two arenas in which the goddess played such a role in the days of the Greeks: war and sports. We have, or at least used to have, Nike missiles, and of course we all know about Nike sports shoes. So in Christ, we are hyper Nikes, or "super winners"—assured of victory in Him.

The promise that nothing can separate us from God

Finally, the ultimate promise is that absolutely nothing in the entire universe, not even death, can separate us from God's love. Paul says, "I am convinced that neither death nor life, neither angels nor demons, neither the present nor the future, nor any powers, neither height nor depth, nor anything else in all creation, will be able to separate us from the love of God that is in Christ Jesus our Lord" (Romans 8:38, 39). It is easy for us to underestimate the power and persistence of God's love, for it seems too good to be true. But nothing in the entire universe is more powerful than God's love, and since God chooses to love us, nothing can separate us from that love.

This list of promises brings the first part of Romans to an end. But don't go away—up to this point Paul has only laid the foundation for what he wants to say. All the good news he has written about so far has important implications for real life, and it is to those implications that Paul will take us now.

---

1. *Siphre Numbers, Shelah* 115:35a, quoted in C. K. Barrett, ed., *The New Testament Background: Selected Documents* (New York: Harper and Row, 1961), 152.

2. The Greek word for patience doesn't have the connotations of inactivity that are sometimes associated with our English word. To wait patiently is not to wait passively; rather, it is to bear up actively under the strain.

3. Notice that Paul doesn't say anyone is predestined for damnation. We'll spend more time on this topic in the next chapter, where we'll study Romans 9.

4. Paul uses the same word here that he used for God handing us over to His wrath back in chapter 1. In other words, we now see how Jesus is the answer to the problem of sin and wrath with which Romans began.

Redemption for Jew and Gentile

Imagine a father who has a son whom he says he loves. He makes all kinds of promises to this son, including the promise that one day everything he owns will belong to the son. He says this son is his beloved heir. But then, for no apparent reason, the father disowns the son, adopts a complete stranger as his son, and makes this adopted stranger the heir. What kind of a father would this be? Certainly not a faithful father. Maybe a capricious father. Maybe an uncaring father. But not a faithful father.

What kind of God would promise the Jews that He would be their God and they would be His people, but then seemed to turn His back on them and adopt the Gentiles instead? Would this be a faithful God? Or would it be a God who reneged on His promises? Did God really choose the Jews as His people? If so, what does Paul's message—that the gospel has gone to the Gentiles—say about God's faithfulness? Paul raised this issue back at the beginning of Romans 3 through a series of rhetorical questions.

What advantage, then, is there in being a Jew, or what value is there in circumcision? Much in every way! First of all, they have been entrusted with the very words of God.

What if some did not have faith? Will their lack of faith

nullify God's faithfulness? Not at all! Let God be true, and every man a liar. As it is written:

> "So that you may be proved right when you speak
>   and prevail when you judge."

But if our unrighteousness brings out God's righteousness more clearly, what shall we say? That God is unjust in bringing his wrath on us? (I am using a human argument.) Certainly not! If that were so, how could God judge the world? (verses 1–6).

Now it is time for Paul to answer these questions in detail. Even the casual reader may notice that there is a change of pace between chapters 8 and 9 of Romans. Many think that the meat of Romans is in chapters 1 through 8 and regard this chapter and those that follow as an appendix that is related but not vital to Paul's argument. But in actual fact, these chapters *are* vital to Paul's message in this letter. He isn't talking just about how individuals are saved; he's concerned about God's reputation. Is God a faithful God who can be trusted? If not, then Paul's entire message is futile. Yet how can God be faithful and trustworthy if He has reneged on His promise to the Jews? What is the advantage of being a Jew if God isn't faithful to His promises? And if He isn't faithful, shouldn't Gentiles beware of putting their trust in Him lest He capriciously change His mind again?

The bottom line

Romans 9–11 is carefully written to address these questions that are so essential to Paul's message. Paul's arguments through this section of his letter aren't easy to follow, and, in fact, may easily be misunderstood. Parts of chapter 9 make God sound very arbitrary and unreasonable. But we shouldn't start on Romans 9 without first taking a brief look at the end of Romans 11. Unless we know where the argument ends up, we can jump to some dangerous conclusions.

So even though this chapter is devoted to Romans 9, we must take a brief look at Romans 11.

Paul's tightly argued discussion in Romans 9–11 ends with a central affirmation. No matter what God has done in history in calling certain people and appearing to reject others, He has always had and continues to have but one goal in mind. His goal is to have mercy on all and to save all. The key is seen in Romans 11:32, 33, "God has imprisoned all in disobedience so that he may be merciful to all. O the depth of the riches and wisdom and knowledge of God! How unsearchable are his judgments and how inscrutable his ways!" (NRSV).

Whenever and whatever God has done, He has had but one goal: to be merciful to all. In other words, He wants to save everyone. We miss the point of Romans 9 completely if we read it without keeping this bottom line in mind. It totally transforms some of what we read and allows us to make sense out of difficult passages in Romans 9. So, with this bottom line constantly in view, we are ready to study Romans 9.

Paul's lament

We have said that Paul is a pastor. Perhaps no passage in Romans makes that more apparent than Romans 9:1–5. Here Paul presents a poignant, personal lament that flows from the depth of his soul. He stresses both that he is telling the truth and that it brings him great sorrow and unceasing anguish. The reason for this sorrow is the condition of his own people, Israel, who for the most part have not accepted the Messiah.

It is hard for Paul to imagine this, given all the blessings that Israel has received. He produces a whole list of these blessings. The list includes

- adoption as God's children;
- divine glory, seen when God revealed Himself on Sinai and in numerous other epiphanies;
- the covenants made with Abraham and renewed continuously to Israel;

90

- the law, which is a gracious blessing even though it cannot save;
- temple worship;
- the promises, of which Christ is the ultimate fulfillment;
- the patriarchs;
- and finally, "according to the flesh"—in other words, in terms of human descent—Christ, the Messiah (NRSV).

With all these privileges, how could anyone in Israel not see what Paul saw in Christ?

Paul's attitude, however, is not one of judgment or condemnation. Rather, he would wish that he could be cursed (a word we still use, *anathema,* which meant "eternally damned") and cut off from Christ if it would mean the salvation of his people. This spirit of solidarity with and concern for his people reminds us of Moses, who, after Israel worshiped the golden calf, said to God, " 'Oh, what a great sin these people have committed! They have made themselves gods of gold. But now, please forgive their sin—but if not, then blot me out of the book you have written' " (Exodus 32:31, 32). There is a difference between these two great pastoral confessions, however. Moses asks to be blotted out *with* the people. Paul, on the other hand, wishes to be shut out *for the sake of* the people. He can't imagine them being lost. He wants to be blotted out so they can be saved.

God's freedom to choose

The remainder of chapter 9 illustrates an Old Testament passage that Paul quotes—Exodus 33:19. When Moses met with God on Sinai, he asked to see God's glory. God said that Moses couldn't see God's face and live, but He would, as Moses had requested, allow him to see His glory. In the course of that conversation God said to Moses, " 'I will have mercy on whom I have mercy, / and I will have compassion on whom I have compassion' " (Romans 9:15, quoting Exodus 33:19). In other words, God is free to do whatever He chooses. He can have mercy on anyone He chooses. Of course, we have to remember the bottom line as given in Romans 11—God's choice is to have mercy on everybody. But for the sake of argument, Paul speaks to those who would question God's faithfulness. They say that the fact that most Jews rejected Jesus as the Messiah makes God unfair. His promise obligates Him to all Jews.

Paul argues, Not so. It has never been true that every literal Jew was part of the promise made to Israel. The Old Testament is full of examples where God has chosen one and not another. God is free and can do whatever He wants. Paul gives several examples of God's freedom from the Scriptures of his Jewish readers:

Isaac and Ishmael (Romans 9:6–9). Abraham had more than one son, but the Jews knew that it was only Isaac and his descendants who were heirs to the promise. This proves that not all natural descendants of Abraham were included in the promise. Verse 7 contains the important word *reckoned,* or considered, that Paul used in Romans 4. Just as righteousness was "reckoned" to Abraham according to chapter 4, Isaac's divine inheritance was "reckoned" by God so that he was a child of promise.

Jacob and Esau (Romans 9:10–15). God chose Jacob as the heir of the promise even though he wasn't the firstborn. He said that He loved Jacob and hated Esau. This point would make sense to the Jews of Paul's day, who didn't consider Esau's descendants as Israel, for they were the Edomites, or Idumeans, whom the Jews neither loved nor embraced.

Pharaoh (Romans 9:17). God raised up Pharaoh for His own purpose. He hardened Pharaoh's heart. This shows that God is free to raise up whomever He chooses.

Hosea (Romans 9:25, 26). Paul quotes two passages from Hosea (2:23; 1:10) to show that God predicted that those who were not His people would be called His people. God is free to choose anyone He wants as His people.

Isaiah (Romans 9:27–29). Paul also quotes two passages from Isaiah (10:22, 23; 1:9) to show that even though there were numerous Israelites, Isaiah had declared that only a remnant of them would be saved. This again shows that not all literal Israelites were children of the promise. If God hadn't kept a remnant, Israel would be like Sodom and Gomorrah, with no one being spared.

All these passages from the Old Testament show that God is free and can choose those He wants as the heirs of His promise. What if someone complains about these examples and wants to press the point of God's unfaithfulness? Paul writes them off by saying, "Who indeed are you, a human being, to argue with God? Will what is molded say to the one who molds it, 'Why have you made me like this?' Has the potter no right over the clay, to make out of the same lump one object for special use and another for ordinary use?" (Romans 9:20, 21, NRSV).

Another point Paul makes is that all of this depends not on human action but on divine choice. He says, "It does not, therefore, depend on man's desire or effort, but on God's mercy" (verse 16).

All this would sound very arbitrary and unfair on the part of God if we were to forget the bottom line of the argument in chapter 11. Yes, God is free to choose, but what He actually does choose is to have mercy on all in the hope of saving all. He doesn't act in an arbitrary and capricious way, even though Paul argues that He has the right to do so. The point here is that God is faithful. In fact, He is more than faithful. He goes beyond what is fair and acts instead on the basis of His mercy and grace.

Paul concludes chapter 9 by quoting once more from Isaiah, this time from chapters 8:14 and 28:16. In these passages, Isaiah speaks of a stumbling block that will come to Israel—but, he says, those who trust God will not stumble. Paul applies this to the Jewish rejection and the Gentile acceptance of Christ by saying,

> What then shall we say? That the Gentiles, who did not pursue righteousness, have obtained it, a righteousness that is by faith; but Israel, who pursued a law of righteousness, has not attained it. Why not? Because they pursued it not by faith but as if it were by works. They stumbled over the "stumbling stone." As it is written:

"See, I lay in Zion a stone that causes men to stumble
and a rock that makes them fall,
and the one who trusts in him will never be put to
shame"(Romans 9:30–33).

It is those who trust—those who have faith—who will escape shame. This will become more apparent as we move on to the rest of the argument in Romans 10 and 11.

CHAPTER 11

The Election of Grace

We could hardly be faulted if we concluded from Romans 9 that God is arbitrary. Just look at the following list of statements that might lead us to that conclusion:

- Verse 13—God loved Jacob and hated Esau.
- Verse 15—God has compassion on whomever He wishes to show compassion.
- Verse 17—God raised Pharaoh up for His own purpose.
- Verse 18—God has mercy on whomever He wishes and hardens the hearts of whomever He wishes.
- Verse 20—Humans have no right to talk back to God.
- Verse 21—God is the Potter who can do whatever He wants to with us, the clay.
- Verse 22—God prepares some for destruction.
- Verse 27—Only a remnant will be saved.

This isn't the picture of God that most of us would like to have. As we noted at the beginning of chapter 10 of this book, these statements make sense only when we get to the bottom line of Paul's tightly woven, three-chapter argument (Romans 9–11). The whole purpose is to show that God is faithful and plans to save *everyone* and show mercy to *all*. That will become clear as we work our way through Romans 10 and 11.

Pursuing righteousness (Romans 10:1-3)

Paul begins chapter 10 as he did chapter 9, by expressing a heart-felt concern for his own people, the Jews. But there's a problem: they have pursued righteousness, but they went about it in the wrong way. They had two major misconceptions: first, they thought they could gain it themselves, and second, they thought it was just for them.

Remember what we said earlier about righteousness—it is more than individual salvation. Although the background of the term is legal, the legal system of Paul's day differs from ours. The judge went out and tried to set right things that were unjust, not as they should be. Just so, God, the true Judge, wants to set everything right. He wants to create a community in which all people live in harmony with Him and with each other. The righteousness He desires is social, not just individual, and universal, not just private.

Paul claims that his people, although zealous for God, don't understand this. He says they want to establish their own righteousness—a righteousness they've created as their private property. He's trying to expand their thinking to see the breadth and depth of God's righteousness, a righteousness that is for everyone.

Christ, the end of the law (Romans 10:4)

In Romans 10:4, Paul says, "Christ is the end of the law so that there may be righteousness for everyone who believes." The Greek word *telos,* like its English counterpart *end,* can have different meanings. When I take a dish out of the dishwasher and it slips out of my hand and breaks into hundreds of pieces on the floor, I can say, "That's the end of that dish!" In this case, *end* means "demise." That dish is no more. But I can also say, "We're raising money at church with the end in mind of a new youth chapel." Here I'm not speaking of the demise of something but of a goal or purpose. So, which meaning of the word did Paul intend when he wrote that Christ is the "end" of the law? Commentators present several possibilities:

1. Christ brings the law to an end. It is now worthless and irrelevant.
2. Christ is the goal toward which the law points. He fulfills the law.
3. Christ brings an end to a misunderstanding of the law.

For evidence that Paul didn't have number 1 in mind, all we have to do is go back and re-read Romans 6–8. Remember that the law "is holy, righteous, and good" (Romans 7:12). What Paul means by *end* is probably a combination of numbers 2 and 3. Christ is the purpose of the law. He is the One to whom the law points. And He brings an end to the exclusivist understanding of the law that saw it as separating the Jews from the Gentiles. According to Romans 10:4, God's goal is to provide, in Christ, righteousness for *everyone* who believes. No longer may anyone use the law to claim righteousness as the private possession of a few.

A Bible study (Romans 10:5-21)

In Romans 10:5–21, Paul quotes a number of passages from the Old Testament.

- Verse 5: The one "who does these things will live by them" (Leviticus 18:5).
- Verses 6–8: "The word is near you"—not something you search for far away (Deuteronomy 30:12–14).
- Verse 11: "Anyone who trusts in [God will not] be put to shame" (Isaiah 28:16).
- Verse 13: "Everyone who calls on the name of the Lord will be saved" (Joel 2:32).
- Verse 15: "How beautiful are the feet of those who bring good news!" (Isaiah 52:7).

- Verse 16: "Lord, who has believed our message?" (Isaiah 53:1).
- Verse 18: "Their voice has gone out into all the earth, / their words to the ends of the world" (Psalm 19:4).
- Verse 19: God will make Israel "envious by those who are not a nation" (Deuteronomy 32:21).
- Verse 20: God "was found by those who did not seek" Him (Isaiah 65:1).
- Verse 21: God has held out His hands "to a disobedient and obstinate people" (Isaiah 65:2).

What is the point of this Bible study? Paul knows the idea that salvation is for everyone may seem strange to some of his Jewish hearers, so he goes back to the Old Testament to show them that in their own Bible God makes the points that He is open to all who trust Him, that everyone can be saved, that He will send His message to those outside Israel, and that Israel has been disobedient. In essence, Paul is using the Jewish Scriptures to show that what he's said in the first four verses isn't novel or heretical; it comes from the Bible itself. God's goal has always been to provide righteousness for *all people*. So, God isn't being unfaithful when He extends His mercy to the Gentiles. If the Jews had really listened, they would have known that God was concerned for more than them alone. God's plan hasn't been to turn away from His children, but to be faithful to the more inclusive vision He has tried to show them all along.

God's amazing plan: To have mercy on all (Romans 11:1-16)

Some Jews, however, might read what Paul has been saying as an affront to them. If God is now reaching out to include Gentiles, doesn't that mean He would be rejecting the very people to whom He made promises? God said Israel would be "His people." Doesn't this movement toward the Gentiles mean He has rejected His people and been unfaithful to His promises?

Paul begins by asking this question, "Did God reject His people?" (Romans 11:1). His answer is yet another of his "Absolutely not!" responses. Like a good attorney, Paul presents evidence: exhibit A and exhibit B.

Exhibit A is Paul himself. He is a Jew. Paul never ceased to consider himself a Jew of the tribe of Benjamin. If God had rejected the Jews, Paul would have been rejected. Instead, he's preaching the good news of God's mercy and grace for all. Therefore, if they will just look at him, they will see that God hasn't rejected Israel.

Exhibit B comes from the Old Testament story of Elijah. As God's prophet, Elijah came to the conclusion that he was the only person left who was faithful to God. But God let him know that there were seven thousand who had not worshiped Baal. God had a remnant that had remained faithful even though the vast majority of Israel had turned from Him. Paul compares that to his own day, in which the majority of Israel has failed to see what God is doing in Christ. Paul says the fact that there's still a faithful remnant reveals that God hasn't rejected His people. This "remnant," Paul said, was "chosen by [God's] grace" (verse 5).

According to Romans 11:7, God hardened the rest of Israel. Here we go again—Paul makes God seem so arbitrary! But now we're getting closer to Paul's presentation of God's ultimate plan—a plan that shows that God isn't arbitrary at all. In verses 8–10, Paul quotes from several Old Testament passages to affirm that Israel has failed (Deuteronomy 29:4; Isaiah 29:10; Psalm 69:22, 23). But in verse 11 he says they haven't fallen beyond recovery. And then, in the next several verses, Paul reveals the amazing plan that God has. It's unbelievable and incredible: *Israel's transgression and rejection of the gospel has led to the gospel being given to the Gentiles. Their acceptance of the gospel will make the Jews envious,*[1] *and through this envy, the Jews will accept the gospel.* Or to put it another way, the Jewish No leads to the Gentile Yes, which, through envy, leads to the Jewish Yes.

Paul knew where he was heading all along. All those pictures that made God look so arbitrary were leading up to this: God isn't arbitrary. He has a plan in mind, and everything He does leads toward that plan. The plan is to save everyone. Whatever God may do along the way, His ultimate goal is to have mercy on *everyone,* Jew and Gentile. God is faithful to Israel. He's also faithful to the Gentiles. He doesn't want to destroy anyone. His goal is mercy for all.

This is almost too good to be true! Paul sees the results as nothing short of eschatological—equivalent to the resurrection of the dead. He summarizes his astonishment in Romans 11:15, "If their [the Jews'] rejection is the reconciliation of the world, what will their acceptance be but life from the dead?"

The olive tree allegory (Romans 11:17-24)

One of the greatest scandals in two thousand years of Christian history has been the mistreatment and persecution of Jews by some Christians. If Christians would only read these verses of Romans, they would halt all Christian anti-Semitism.

Remember, Paul is writing as a pastor. The difficulty of his argument in these three chapters tempts us to forget that. But all of his argument has to do with real issues in the church at Rome. When Paul is writing, most of the church at Rome is Gentile. That is certainly a change from when the church began there. It undoubtedly started as a church made up totally of Jewish Christians. How should the present Gentile majority in the church treat its Jewish minority? Paul draws again from the Old Testament to send a very clear message about how Jews and Gentiles should get along in the church.

In the Old Testament, Israel was often compared to a tree. The kind of tree could vary. It could be an oak (Isaiah 61:3) or a cedar (Psalm 92:12). But in Jeremiah 11:16, 17, Israel is compared to an olive tree, and Paul probably had this passage in mind when he wrote Romans 11:17–24, since both Jeremiah and Paul speak of Israel's unfaithfulness in terms of branches being broken off. Jeremiah says,

> The LORD called you a thriving olive tree
> with fruit beautiful in form.

But with the roar of a mighty storm
    he will set it on fire,
    and its branches will be broken.

The LORD Almighty, who planted you, has decreed disaster for you, because the house of Israel and the house of Judah have done evil and provoked me to anger by burning incense to Baal.

In Paul's allegory, the root of the tree is God, who supports all the branches. The natural branches are the Jews, and the wild branches are the Gentiles. Paul compares the breaking off of some of the branches of the olive tree as the consequence of the rejection of the gospel by some of the Jews. Those who rejected it have been broken off and replaced by Gentile Christians—they're like the wild branches grafted into the olive tree. But now Paul warns the Gentiles—the wild branches who've been grafted in—not to get bigheaded and begin looking down on the Jews. They're not to brag about being grafted in, for if God could cut off natural branches, He certainly could also cut off the wild branches. And if God could graft in wild branches, He certainly could re-graft in the natural branches that have been cut off. So no one should be proud.

Apparently, some Gentiles were tempted to be conceited and look down on the Jews who had rejected the gospel. Their prideful attitude toward the Jews is evidence of their failure to understand that God's mercy is for everyone—not just Gentiles, but Jews as well.

This picture of God's continuing concern for and commitment to the Jews demolishes anti-Semitism. No true Christian can look down on one of these Jews whom God continues to love.

Mercy for all (Romans 11:25-32)

Paul now reiterates the amazing plan that God has revealed. Israel has experienced a hardening until the full number of Gentiles has come in. This probably doesn't mean a specific quantity of Gentiles, but rather looks to a time when the gospel has gone to those who need to hear it throughout the Gentile world. But then Paul says that "all Israel will be saved" (Romans 11:26). This has been a very controversial statement. Does Paul mean it literally—that every Jew will be saved? Probably not. But clearly, it is God's plan to save all Israel. We shouldn't dismiss this statement too quickly. Paul says in verse 29 that "God's gifts and his call are irrevocable." I get the idea that Paul saw God's commitment of grace to the Jews and to us as something much stronger and more tenacious than we usually consider it to be. God's grace is so persistent that He will do everything He possibly can to save every single person, Jew and Gentile.

The conclusion of this difficult, three-chapter argument is clear. God has bound everyone over to disobedience for one purpose and one purpose only: His desire is to have mercy on *all*. Not just Jews. Not just Gentiles. Not even just some Jews and some Gentiles. His goal is mercy for all.

Doxology

When Paul tries to grasp the meaning of God's plan, he can only stand back in wonder and sing a doxology—a hymn of praise to God. Romans 9–11 may present challenges of interpretation. But it doesn't end in theology. It ends in worship. God's amazing plan, the persistence of His grace, and the depth of His love are all so wonderful that Paul can only break into song. And to comment on such a song is only to detract from it. What we ought to do is sing it with Paul:

> Oh, the depth of the riches of the wisdom and knowledge of God!
>> How unsearchable his judgments,
>> and his paths beyond tracing out!
> "Who has known the mind of the Lord?
>> Or who has been his counselor?"
> "Who has ever given to God,
>> that God should repay him?"

For from him and through him and to him are all things.
To him be the glory forever! Amen (Romans 11:33–36).

---

1. Notice the word *envious* in the quote from Deuteronomy 32:21.

CHAPTER 12

Love and Law

One of the most important words in the book of Romans comes at the beginning of Romans 12. It's the word *therefore*. It's important because it ties what Paul is about to say in the final chapters of Romans with what he has already said in the first eleven chapters.

Why is this important? Some claim that Paul's message of righteousness by faith is actually inconsistent with what he says about Christian behavior. They argue that Paul tacks on ethical advice at the end of his letters out of tradition, but this practical advice has nothing to do with his basic message. The word *therefore* refutes this. The last part of Paul's letter grows logically out of the theological message he has presented. In fact, this practical advice is what the whole message has been leading up to. In light of all that Paul has said theologically, "therefore"—and he goes on to tell us how we should live. This transition from the theological to the practical with the word *therefore* is typical of Paul's letters.

- Romans 12:1—Therefore, present your bodies as living sacrifices.
- Galatians 5:1—Therefore, stand fast in the freedom for which Christ set you free.
- Ephesians 4:1—Therefore, live worthy of your calling.

- 1 Thessalonians 4:1—Therefore, learn more and more how to please God.
- 2 Thessalonians 2:15—Therefore, stand fast in holding on to what you have been taught.

Paul moves from the theoretical to the practical by saying "therefore" because he wants to show the connection between the two. He is saying, "God has done a lot for us, therefore, this is how we should live."

A living sacrifice (Romans 12:1, 2)

As Paul begins focusing on the practical issues of everyday living, he makes a request of the Romans by using a formula called an appeal statement. Writers frequently used such statements when they were attempting to elicit a specific response from the readers. The formula went like this:

"I urge you, (a), by (b), to (c)."
    (a) = the person to whom the appeal is addressed
    (b) = the basis for the appeal
    (c) = the desired response

In our case, (a) is the Roman believers, (b) is God's mercy, and (c) is that the Romans present their bodies as living sacrifices to God. The whole first eleven chapters have stressed God's mercy. Now, on the basis of the amazing mercy that God has poured out on us, the appropriate response is for us to give our bodies as living sacrifices to God.

The background of this request is the sacrificial system of worship that prevailed in both the Judaism and the pagan religions of Paul's day. God, of course, had asked Israel to sacrifice in the temple. The book of Leviticus contains all kinds of rules regarding sacrifices that served various purposes. The first five books of the Bible portray God as pleased with such sacrifices. Notice what Genesis 8:20, 21, says about the sacrifice that Noah offered. "Noah built an altar to the LORD and, taking some of all the clean animals and clean birds, he sacrificed burnt offerings on it. The LORD smelled the pleasing aroma and said in his heart: 'Never again will I curse the ground because of man, even though every inclination of his heart is evil from childhood.' "

But the prophets emphasized the other side of the coin—the danger of offering sacrifices as a mere ritual without a corresponding change in the heart and life. So in Micah 6:6–8, the prophet asks,

> With what shall I come before the LORD
>   and bow down before the exalted God?
> Shall I come before him with burnt offerings,
>   with calves a year old?
> Will the LORD be pleased with thousands of rams,
>   with ten thousand rivers of oil?
> Shall I offer my firstborn for my transgression,
>   the fruit of my body for the sin of my soul?
> He has showed you, O man, what is good.
>   And what does the LORD require of you?
> To act justly and to love mercy
>   and to walk humbly with your God.

Paul stands in line with the prophets and asks that worship be a matter of the heart. For him, the true, spiritual worship that God desires is our entire life—the whole person (this is what he means by "body") given to God. This is what it means to be a living sacrifice. We give ourselves to God, not to be cast into the image of this present evil age, but to be transformed according to the values and principles of God's kingdom. This happens as our minds are renewed by our fellowship with God and by the Spirit living in us. Paul will go on in the rest of this letter to show us the shape of this renewed mind that lives as a sacrifice to God.

Only three times in this letter does Paul use an appeal statement to make a specific request of the Romans—here in Romans 12:1; in Romans 15:30, where he asks the Romans to pray on his behalf; and in Romans 16:17, where he asks them to be on guard against those who would cause divisions in their church.

The body of Christ (Romans 12:3-8)

The first way that we present our body as a living sacrifice to God is by being part of Christ's body on the earth. In order to serve in the body of Christ, we need to have a realistic assessment of our abilities.

Paul starts this section with a play on words. He uses three words from the same root: *phroneo,* "to think"; *huperphroneo,* to "hyperthink"—to think too highly of oneself, to be haughty; and *sophroneo,* "to think sensibly or wisely." Paul urges the Romans to think sensibly, not haughtily. In other words, they are to have an accurate assessment of themselves.

We often call this assessment of our abilities *self-awareness.* Many times when we speak of self-awareness, however, it's in the context of an individualistic, even self-centered effort to understand ourselves. For Paul, the goal of self-awareness is service. We need to understand ourselves and our gifts so we will know how to serve.

These gifts are not merely natural endowments but are part of the measure of faith that God gives. He gives diverse gifts so that the body will have different kinds of members for different kinds of service. Yet, while each member performs a different kind of service, each "belongs to all the others" (verse 5). Even though the members have different functions, they are part of one body. Each one works in harmony with the whole.

The list of gifts that Paul gives here is hardly exhaustive. The gifts are prophesying (by which Paul didn't mean predicting the future but preaching the gospel under the Spirit's inspiration), serving (we get our term *deacon* from the Greek root of this word), teaching, encouraging, contributing to the needs of others, leadership, and showing mercy. Paul admonishes those who have received these gifts to use them diligently in accordance with the faith God has given.

Notice how strongly these gifts focus on building up both the spiritual life and the sense of community among believers. Notice, too, that these gifts that build up the church aren't limited to clergy or super-Christians. They include simple acts such as encouraging each other (perhaps with a smile or a note), contributing to the needy, serving, and showing mercy. We've probably put too much emphasis on gifts that belong to a few leaders and not enough on the everyday, practical gifts that do the most to build up the body of Christ. I'm sure that many people go home from church blessed more by a smile than by a sermon.

This emphasis on the body of Christ is sometimes difficult for people in my Southern California culture, which is very individualistic. We all drive our own cars—we're too independent for car pools or mass transit. And we carry this over into our religion. Christianity is seen as just me and Jesus, no need for a church. But Paul couldn't conceive of a relationship with Christ that doesn't include participation in Christ's body, for it's in the body that the righteousness of God becomes a reality.

The shape of love (Romans 12:9-21)

Verses 9–13 seem to focus on what love looks like within the community of believers. Paul's word for love here is *agape,* the self-giving and unselfish concern for others. The snippets of advice Paul gives in verses 10–13 seem to spin out of his mouth one after the other with little context. In the original language, those snippets have a kind of parallelism that the English translator can hardly capture. Here's my attempt to catch the structure, but you'll notice that to do so means to sacrifice some of the English meaning. Literally, verses 10–13 could be translated as the following:

In brotherly love for one another, devoting yourselves,
in honor for each other, leading out,
in haste, not being lazy,
in the spirit, boiling,
in the Lord, serving,
in hope, rejoicing,
in affliction, enduring,

in prayer, persisting,
in the needs of the saints, sharing.

Verses 14–21 seem to focus on what love looks like as we reach outside of our own community to others who aren't Christian. This advice is quite reminiscent of the Sermon on the Mount in Matthew 5–7 and also has several parallels to the advice found in 1 Peter. It may be that this was typical advice given to new Christians when they were baptized.

The advice centers on living at peace with others and not seeking revenge when one is persecuted. Paul realizes that we don't always control others, so he says we should live at peace with others as far as possible—"as far as it depends on you" (Romans 12:18). Paul ends this section by quoting from Proverbs 25:21, 22. No one can say for sure what heaping coals of fire on someone's head means, but probably it signifies trying to lead them to repentance by our kindness, for putting coals of fire on one's head was often a sign of repentance.

This advice that Paul gives goes against the grain of some of the most popular philosophy of the day. The Stoics taught that one should keep an attitude of detachment to avoid being hurt. One of them said that even when you hugged your children you should remember that they are mortal and might be gone tomorrow,[1] and that when you mourn with someone, you should mourn only on the outside, not in the center of your being.[2] But Paul says we should rejoice with those who rejoice and mourn with those who mourn. Christians open their hearts to others even at the risk of pain.

Christians and the emperor (Romans 13:1-7)

There are at least two reasons why the advice Paul gives about submitting to the civil authorities seems confusing. First, Paul emphasizes that the authorities are a threat only to bad behavior. If you do only good things, you don't have to worry about them. This seems a bit strange coming from the mouth of someone who was beaten and imprisoned by the authorities over and over again.

Notice what Paul says he's experienced. "Five times I received from the Jews the forty lashes minus one. Three times I was beaten with rods, once I was stoned, three times I was shipwrecked, I spent a night and a day in the open sea, I have been constantly on the move. I have been in danger from rivers, in danger from bandits, in danger from my own countrymen, in danger from Gentiles; in danger in the city, in danger in the country, in danger at sea; and in danger from false brothers" (2 Corinthians 11:24–26). And several of Paul's letters mention that he was writing from prison (Ephesians, Philippians, Colossians, Philemon, and 2 Timothy). How can one who was so often at odds with the law and the authorities speak so positively about them?

Second, in many ways, Paul's whole message in Romans seems to be subversive of these very authorities. Remember that the Roman emperors often claimed divine privilege and demanded that their subjects bow to them as lord. The language of Romans stands in stark contrast to the claims of the Roman establishment. The following are some examples:

- When Roman emperors announced the celebrations of their birthdays and other special occasions, they referred to the announcements as "gospels." They were announcements of good news. But nine times in this letter Paul speaks of the gospel as the good news of salvation by God's grace.
- The emperors were fond of calling themselves "lord." Paul calls Jesus Christ "Lord" forty-three times in Romans alone.
- The emperors emphasized that they were the ones who brought righteousness and peace. For Paul, it is God through Jesus who brings both righteousness and peace.

Certainly, Christians who knew what the emperor was saying would catch the contrast and recognize that Paul was calling them to a different worldview than that espoused by the emperors. Surely, they must have caught the fact that Paul was calling them to give only to Christ the allegiance that was usually given to the emperors.

Yet Paul also calls Christians to submit to the governing authorities. Here's the essence of what he says—Christians are to submit to the authorities for two reasons. First, those authorities have been put in their positions by God. This doesn't mean every individual leader is God's choice, but that God has ordained that there be governments to prevent chaos. Second, the authorities are a threat only to those who do evil. The first reason is theological, and the second is pragmatic. Then Paul repeats these two reasons in opposite order. Christians should submit to authorities to avoid punishment (the pragmatic) and because of conscience (the theological) (see Romans 13:5).

Why doesn't Paul talk about the exceptions here? Why doesn't he say that sometimes the authorities persecute Christians and act in ways that are anything but just? We can't know for sure, but probably Paul was giving more general advice here, just as Peter did in 1 Peter 2:13–17. Possibly, this was fairly standard advice given to new Christian converts at the time of their baptism (see what follows), and Paul didn't feel he had to talk about all the possible exceptions at this point.

It's true of both the early Christians and us that on most days we aren't confronting major decisions about standing up for our faith against government opposition. We're much more likely to be tempted to ignore the government's legitimate claims by cheating on our taxes or breaking the speed limit. That is probably why Paul emphasizes the basic principle without going into all the exceptions. We do owe the government taxes for the services it provides, and we owe general obedience to avoid anarchy. There are plenty of places in the world where anarchy does exist, and it isn't a pretty sight.

The priority of love (Romans 13:8-10)

When Jesus was asked about the greatest commandment, He gave a twofold answer: "One of the teachers of the law came and heard them debating. Noticing that Jesus had given them a good answer, he asked him, 'Of all the commandments, which is the most important?' 'The most important one,' answered Jesus, 'is this: "Hear, O Israel, the Lord our God, the Lord is one. Love the Lord your God with all your heart and with all your soul and with all your mind and with all your strength." The second is this: "Love your neighbor as yourself." There is no commandment greater than these' " (Mark 12:28–31).[3]

Unlike Jesus, Paul sums up the law with just one command—Jesus' second one: " 'Love your neighbor as yourself' " (Romans 13:9). He does this not only here in Romans, but also in Galatians 5:14, 15. Why does it take Jesus two commands when it takes Paul only one?

In part, this may just be a matter of Paul's language preference. While he uses the word *love* for God's attitude toward us and our attitude toward others, he seems to prefer the term *faith* for our attitude toward God. Romans 8:28 is the only place in Romans where Paul speaks of us loving God.

Paul says the only debt we owe is the debt of love, and love fulfills the entire law. In Romans 7:6, he wrote about serving "not in the old way of the written code," but in the Spirit. He wants to see Christians live in obedience to the law not just because they feel constrained to do so, but because the Spirit has put love in their hearts and it's natural to express it. In other words, Paul would hope that you wouldn't steal your neighbor's car because you love your neighbor so much that you wouldn't want to take what is his. That is much better than continuing to want to steal but refraining from doing so just because the law forbids it. If we are truly motivated by love, we won't want to harm others.

So if we have love, do we even need the law? Even though love motivates us to want to do what is good for our neighbor, we still need the gracious instruction God gives us to make sure that we know the shape of love. God's instruction in the law shows us what true love for others actually means and keeps us from justifying our own selfishness in the name of love.

Night and day (Romans 13:11-14)

Paul concludes this chapter with an analogy about night and day and sleeping and waking. He compares our present life in this world with night, and the coming of Christ when the fullness of salvation is revealed with day. He also compares the works of evil with night and the works of good with day. The metaphor gains part of its power from the fact that evil works are often done in shame, and therefore, also in secret, shrouded in darkness. These deeds of the night are "orgies and drunkenness, . . . sexual immorality and debauchery, . . . dissension and jealousy" (Romans 13:13), and are synonymous with the desires of the flesh. In contrast, the new world to come is a world of light where good works and openness prevail. Therefore, it is appropriately symbolized by the light of the day. Paul calls on us to begin living now as in the day. Salvation is just around the corner, and the Christian, who already sees the first rays of dawn, begins now to live in the day—in other words, to live now according to the values of God's eternal kingdom.

Paul is fond of this metaphor of light and darkness. He uses it in 1 Thessalonians 5:1–11 too. And there, too, it's tied to both eschatology and proper Christian living. Some people argue that belief in Christ's soon coming weakens the motivation to behave ethically. If Christ is coming soon, why bother about trying to help others by making this world better? Why bother with working for the good of others? Paul takes exactly the opposite view. He says that the Christian belief that Christ is coming soon should motivate them to live now according to the values of justice, compassion, and love that characterize God's coming kingdom.

Paul closes chapter 13 by calling Christians to clothe themselves with Christ (see verse 14). This kind of language appears to be associated with Christian baptism. We see it in Galatians 3:27, where Paul says, "All of you who were baptized into Christ have clothed yourselves with Christ." He then goes on to express the oneness of all in Christ. In Colossians 3:10–12, we find the same expression of oneness tied with the language of clothing. Apparently, when Christians were baptized, they thought of themselves as being clothed

113

with a new life—that of Christ Himself. To put on Christ is another metaphor for accepting Christ's values and living according to His love and compassion. Paul contrasts this with gratifying the desires of the flesh (Romans 13:14), which reminds us of what he said in Romans 7:5 and 8:5–8. All of this strengthens the likelihood that the instructions in Romans 12 and 13 are typical of the instructions given to new Christians.

Paul's advice in chapters 12 and 13 gives shape to the life of love. It shows us what it means to live a life that is a living sacrifice to God and to already be transformed into the life of the future age of salvation. And the "therefore" at the beginning of chapter 12 shows that this advice is integrally related to all that has gone before in Romans. The righteousness that God is revealing in the world through Jesus results in a new community of believers. These believers are diverse, made up of Jew and Gentile and all kinds of people with different gifts. But they are one in Christ. They live in this world, but they already live life according to the values of the next world, which is about to dawn.

---

1. Epictetus, *Enchiridion* 3.
2. Ibid., 16.
3. Jesus' quotations come from Deuteronomy 6:4, 5 and Leviticus 19:18.

What It's Really All About

Once when I worked as an administrator in an Adventist college, an accrediting team came to determine if we were being faithful to our mission. When the visiting team held its initial meeting with the administrators, one member told us what he intended to do. He said he was going to go into the men's shower room on Sabbath morning when it was time for Sabbath School to see if students were showering when they should have been in the church. He also said he would stand at the end of the cafeteria line and look at the trays to see if students were eating according to proper health standards— no cheese, for instance. He added that he would do these and similar things because he believed the most important mark of true spirituality is the way we relate to standards.

I'm not sure Paul would agree. The believers in Rome were divided over certain standards. No doubt some of them were hoping that Paul would set the record straight and let them know what the correct standard of behavior was for all of them. But he didn't do that. Instead, he told them there was something more important than how they related to standards. What was more important was how they related to God and to each other.

This advice was anything but a nonessential appendix added to the essential message of the gospel. This is the climax of the book. This is what Paul had been leading up to all along. The message of salvation by grace through faith is not just a theoretical formula to be believed. It is a message to be lived out in a community of believers. Now we get to see how that should work. Now we reach the part of the letter to the Romans that tells us what the letter is really all about.

The weak and the strong (Romans 14:1-15:13)

Paul begins chapter 14 with the admonition to welcome those who are weak in the faith. Who are these people? They are those who are more strict or scrupulous with regard to certain standards. They eat only vegetables, and they consider certain days to be special. In Romans 15:1, Paul identifies himself with the strong—presumably, those who are less strict on these matters.

Apparently, the Christians in Rome were divided over these matters of food and days. Unfortunately, Paul doesn't give us a lot of detail about the issues of concern. As we will see, he's far less interested in the issues than in how people relate to each other. But first, let's look at what we *can* say about the situation in Rome.

Whatever the debate over food was all about, the issue was probably not food that had been offered to idols. In 1 Corinthians 8–10 that is clearly the issue. Although in Romans, Paul gives many of the same principles that he gave to the Corinthians, in this letter he doesn't make any specific reference to food offered to idols. In Corinthians, Paul is very specific in the terms he uses that refer to eating food offered to idols. The absence of these terms in Romans indicates the issue there must have been different.

There were various reasons in Paul's day that a person might have chosen not to eat meat. For instance, in the Gentile world, the reasons included cultic ritual, denial of pleasure, rejection of luxury, health, belief in the transmigration of souls, and avoidance of cruelty to animals. We simply do not know what motivated these "weak" Romans.

In Romans 14:14, Paul also raises the issue of clean and unclean. Whether that was also part of the dispute in Rome or he was simply giving general advice is hard to say. In either case, when Paul says that nothing "is unclean in itself," he isn't saying that everything is good for you to eat. In the first century, many still believed in an inherent distinction between clean and unclean that meant you were ritually unclean even if you just touched certain things, and Paul no longer believed in this ritualistic understanding of clean and unclean distinctions.

As for the days that were under dispute, Paul doesn't give us much to go on. He simply says that some people esteem or "consider" days. The New International Version translation is quite misleading when it says, "One man considers one day more sacred than another" (Romans 14:5). The original text says nothing about days being "sacred." This is an interpretive addition to the text. The New Revised Standard Version is better when it says, "Some judge one day to be better than another." The issue does not appear to be about sacred days or worship days. It would be inconceivable that in the first century, some Christians in Rome considered all days alike and had no worship day.

Since the context is food, the best guess is that the "days" also involved eating. Some were probably fasting on certain days, and others didn't fast on a regular basis. Remember, Jesus chided the Pharisees for their fasting, yet we know that fasting was still carried out in parts of the early church. For example, the book of Christian teaching called the *Didache* tells Christians not to fast like the hypocrites (it's referring to Jews) who fast on the second and fifth days of the week. Instead, it says that Christians should fast on the fourth and sixth days of the week (chapter 8). Most likely the debate in Rome was all about food—what to eat and when to eat it.

Paul's concern, however, is not the specifics of the debate. It's how the people on either side of the debate relate to each other. According to Paul, Christians on both sides seem to have their problems. The stricter Christians were tempted to point the finger of judgment toward those who weren't as strict. After all, the less strict didn't take the standards of behavior as seriously as their critics did—an obvious sign of "inferior" spirituality. On the other hand, the less strict didn't have the problem of judging; their tendency was to look down with scorn on the poor misguided legalists who worried too much about standards of behavior. So each side had its own kind of hostility toward the other. The strict judged the less strict; the less strict scorned the strict. It's this tension between the two that troubles Paul.

The tension probably troubles him for two reasons, one theological and one pragmatic. First, it contradicts the gospel. The goal of the gospel is a community of believers united in Christ and serving as a witness to the world. The gospel is thwarted when Christians aren't united. And second, Paul wants to use Rome as the support base for his mission to Spain. A divided church isn't going to be a very strong support base.

We might wonder why Paul uses the terms *weak* for the more strict and *strong* for the less strict. Perhaps there are at least two reasons. The more strict are more vulnerable to being wounded by the actions of the strong. There is also evidence that the term *weak* was used in the common parlance of the day for the very scrupulous, without the negative connotations that we associate with the term.[1]

In Romans 15:1, Paul clearly identifies with the strong, but he is in no way trying to get everyone to take his position. In fact, he very carefully avoids that. He has advice particularly for the weak and advice particularly for the strong and advice for both. The following lists summarize Paul's advice to each group. Look at the lists, and then we'll summarize what Paul is getting at.

To the Weak

- Don't judge the strong. You are not to judge other people's servants, and the strong are God's servants (Romans 14:3, 4, 10–13).
- Don't violate your convictions. If you have doubts about something, don't do it (verse 23).

To the Strong

- Don't look down on the weak with scorn (Romans 14:3, 10).

- Don't put a stumbling block in the way of another person (verse 13).
- Don't injure a person for whom Christ died (verse 15).
- It's wrong to make your brother or sister fall by what you do (verses 20, 21).
- Put up with the failings of the weak and don't please yourselves (Romans 15:1).

To Both

- Welcome each other, and not just to argue; welcome each other as Christ welcomed you (Romans 14:1; 15:7).
- Let each be fully convinced in his or her own mind (Romans 14:5).
- Remember that the kingdom of God is not a matter of food and drink, but of righteousness, peace, and joy (verse 17).
- Pursue what makes for peace and builds up the community (verse 19).
- Keep your convictions to yourself (verse 22).
- Whatever is not of faith is sin (verse 23).
- Please your neighbor for the sake of building up your neighbor (Romans 15:2).
- Live in harmony with each other (verse 5).
- Abound in hope and be full of joy (verse 13).

These lists give us a pretty good idea of Paul's real concern. His goal is for all to live together in unity, wherever they stand on the specific behaviors in question. He's quite willing to let each group be fully convinced in their own minds; he isn't trying to get everyone into one camp or the other. This probably frustrated some people. I can hear some of the Roman believers saying, "Paul, just give us the right answer. Both ways can't be right! Tell us what to do." But Paul resists. Obviously, this wouldn't be true of all behavioral issues. When there was a case of incest in the Corinthian church, Paul didn't say, "Let each be fully convinced in their own minds."

119

In that case, he told them exactly what to do! (See 1 Corinthians 5.) But Paul doesn't consider the practices in this dispute to involve basic moral issues. And where no basic moral issue is involved, Paul considers the real question to be how the believers will relate to each other.

So the weak aren't to judge the strong, for God alone is Judge. To usurp His role is a spiritual danger. They aren't to judge—but to welcome. But they're also to be true to their convictions. To do what one believes God has forbidden is to go against God. The weak may be mistaken as to what God demands, but they shouldn't violate their understanding of God's will for their lives. To do so would be to violate their relationship with God.

The strong, on the other hand, should adjust their behavior to make sure they don't injure the weak. To refrain from doing what they think acceptable is not to violate their convictions. It isn't even an assault on their freedom. Rather, it shows that they are so free that they don't have to exercise their freedom at the expense of someone else. So they aren't to look down with scorn on the weak, but they're to be sensitive to the convictions of the weak and to make sure they themselves aren't just out to please themselves. If their actions will injure the weak, for the sake of the weak they should be strong enough to give up what they believe is legitimate.

Both groups are to welcome each other. Romans 14:1 and 15:7 bracket this whole discussion with the notion of being welcoming. To be welcoming is more than to be tolerant. It grows out of our gratitude that God has welcomed us. God welcomes even the people who disagree with us—can we do less than welcome them as well?

So, we are to pursue what makes for peace and harmony and what builds up the community. The phrase *to build up* is a favorite of Paul's. He uses it (in the original Greek) four times in Ephesians, nine times in the Corinthian letters, and twice here in this discussion (14:19; 15:2). The goal is to live in harmony, in peace, and with joy. Notice the following verses, which conclude this discussion of the Romans believers' dispute over food and days. Paul makes no reference to either food or days. Instead, he zeros in on the issue of living together in peace and joy. He emphasizes that this includes both Jew and Gentile, quoting from several Old Testament passages that show that the Gentiles are to be included in the joy (2 Samuel 22:50; Psalm 18:49; Deuteronomy 32:43; Psalm 117:1; and Isaiah 11:10). These paragraphs sum up the goal of Paul's message in Romans:

Welcome one another, therefore, just as Christ has welcomed you, for the glory of God. For I tell you that Christ has become a servant of the circumcised on behalf of the truth of God in order that he might confirm the promises given to the patriarchs, and in order that the Gentiles might glorify God for his mercy. As it is written,

"Therefore I will confess you among the Gentiles,
    and sing praises to your name";
and again he says,
    "Rejoice, O Gentiles, with his people";
and again,
    "Praise the Lord, all you Gentiles,
        and let all the peoples praise him";
and again Isaiah says,
    "The root of Jesse shall come,
        the one who rises to rule the Gentiles;
in him the Gentiles shall hope."

May the God of hope fill you with all joy and peace in believing, so that you may abound in hope by the power of the Holy Spirit (Romans 15:7–13, NRSV).

Paul's ministry and plans (Romans 15:14-33)

I wrote about this section in the first chapter of this book, so I'll say little about it here. We saw there how Paul's commitment to take the collection to Jerusalem caused him to travel hundreds of extra miles and kept him from following his plan to go to Spain. We also saw that Paul had concerns about how he would be received in Jerusalem and that he implored the Romans to pray on his behalf. Finally, we saw that Paul considered himself an apostle to the Gentiles, and in chapter 2, we explored what that meant.

One thing we didn't notice earlier was that Paul told his Romans readers that he had spoken rather boldly to them in some matters (Romans 15:15). This was probably a rhetorical device that he used because he was writing to a church he had never visited and he had a specific goal in mind. When compared to letters like 1 and 2 Corinthians and Galatians, Romans hardly seems bold. Paul is quite gentle, even as he pursues the matters that divided the Romans. But some people probably questioned why he should be writing to the Romans at all, and this brief apology is his way of showing that he isn't trying to be presumptuous.

Real people (Romans 16)

If you were asked to name what must be the most boring book in the entire world to read, you might answer it's the white pages of the telephone directory. Imagine just reading name after name after name! The sixteenth chapter of Romans is primarily a couple lists of names, and most readers probably just skip through it because it seems about as interesting as reading the telephone book. But these names represent people, real people, and there are interesting stories behind each one. Unfortunately, we don't know most of these stories, but the little bit we do know about some of these people whets our appetite to learn more. If the final goal of righteousness by faith is a community of believers that lives in harmony with God and with each other, then lists of believers are a fitting way to end a book intended to move people toward that goal.

There are five parts to Romans 16: (1) Paul's recommendation of Phoebe; (2) greetings to various members of the church in Rome; (3) a request and a warning; (4) greetings from Paul's companions; and (5) the final benediction.

Paul's recommendation of Phoebe

Paul begins this final chapter by commending Phoebe to the Romans. He writes from Corinth, and she is from Cenchrae, which was the seaport on the east side of Corinth. It was probably Phoebe who carried the letter from Corinth to Rome. There was no mail service for the general population in Paul's day, so each letter had to be carried by a messenger. She probably would have also been the one who read the letter to the Romans.

It isn't certain what Paul calls Phoebe. Some translations (for example, the King James Version, the New International Version) call her a servant, but others (for example, the New Revised Standard Version) call her a deacon. The term is the word used for deacons in the New Testament, but it is also used more generally for servants, as when Paul calls himself a servant of the new covenant (2 Corinthians 3:6) and of the gospel (Colossians 1:23). Since Paul adds "of the church" after this word, he's probably using the word to say that she is a deacon (Romans 16:1). There's no feminine ending on the word, so it would be wrong to translate this word "deaconess." We'll see throughout this chapter the importance Paul accorded to the matter of women in ministry. Phoebe isn't merely a servant, but a church leader—Paul instructed the Romans to do what she required and to take care of her needs. Perhaps she was already beginning to make preparations for Paul's anticipated trip to Spain.

Greetings to various members of the church in Rome

There was a time when many commentators on Romans didn't believe that this chapter was a part of the original letter to Rome. They thought it might have been written to another congregation, such as Ephesus. They couldn't imagine that Paul would know so many people in Rome since at the time he wrote, he hadn't been there yet. But in the first century, all roads really did lead to Rome. It isn't surprising that many who were in Rome at the time of Paul's writing might have lived in or visited other parts of the empire and met Paul in those places. I won't mention all of these people, but only those whose stories we know something about.

Prisca[2] and Aquila (verses 3–5). We saw in the first chapter of this book that according to Acts 18, this couple met Paul in Corinth after they had been kicked out of Rome by the emperor Claudius. Later, they traveled with Paul to Ephesus and stayed there to work for a while. Now they're back in Rome and a church meets in their house. In the first century, Christians didn't have church buildings. They met in homes. Notice that Paul mentions Prisca's name first, suggesting that she may actually have been the leader of this house church.

Paul says that Prisca and Aquila risked their necks for him, probably when they were working together in Corinth. This may just be a figure of speech, but it may also suggest that they were Roman citizens, since only Roman citizens would be beheaded.

Andronicus and Junia (verse 7). They were probably a married couple, since the name Andronicus is masculine and Junia is feminine. Paul says they were relatives (was this literal or figurative?), were in prison with him at some point, and were apostles before he was. Thus, we have here the case of a female apostle. Paul refers to several other women who were workers with him. Again, we see that women played an important part in the ministry in the early church.

Those of the household of Aristobulus (verse 10) and the household of Narcissus (verse 11). Paul is probably speaking of slaves and free servants who worked in the households of these two people. The name *Aristobulus* suggests that this man had an aristocratic Jewish background. *Narcissus* was a woman's name often used by former slaves. Possibly neither of these heads of households or estates were Christians, but a number of their slaves and former slaves were. Each of these groups probably made up a separate house church that met with the permission of their masters.

Rufus (verse 13). This is probably the most intriguing name on the list because of the story that may stand behind it. Rufus was a common name, so just because it occurs twice in the New Testament doesn't necessarily mean that the two occurrences refer to the same person. However, there's good evidence that they might. Rufus is also mentioned in Mark 15:21, where we learn that he was the son of Simon of Cyrene, who carried the cross of Jesus. It's unlikely that Mark would have mentioned the names of Simon's sons unless he knew that his readers were acquainted with them. The tradition is that Mark wrote his Gospel for believers in Rome about a decade after Paul sent his letter. So if Mark expected those in Rome to know who Rufus was, this may well be the same Rufus. The truly intriguing part of the story is that Paul says Rufus's mother was also his mother. This is undoubtedly figurative; he probably meant that she was like a mother to him. But if Mark's Rufus was also Paul's Rufus, this suggests that Simon of Cyrene, who carried Jesus' cross merely because he was compelled to, became a Christian and had two sons (one of whom was known in Rome to both Paul and Mark) and a wife who was like a mother to Paul. Wouldn't you love to know whether all this was true?

In verses 14 and 15, Paul lists two groups of names, greets them, and then adds greetings to the brothers and sisters who are with them. Here he may be referring to two different house churches. So, we may have seen at least five different house churches in this chapter. Probably the most one could fit in a house church would be about seventy-five people. Of course, there may have been other house churches that Paul doesn't mention.

A request and a warning

In verses 17–20, Paul makes his third specific request of the Romans. (The first two are in Romans 12:1 and 15:30.) He asks them "to watch out for those who cause divisions" and teach contrary to what they have learned (verse 17). This is the first warning in the letter against false teachers. Did Paul know of some specific group that was coming to Rome, or was this simply general advice because he knew that such people might show up anywhere? We really can't know for sure. These people who talk flattery but really serve their own appetites remind us of similar warnings Paul will later give to the Philippian believers (see Philippians 3). Paul also assures the Romans that soon Jesus will crush the power of Satan under their feet.

Greetings from Paul's companions

Paul not only greets those in Rome, but he sends greetings from those who are with him in the area of Corinth. These are people who would probably have been close to Paul. He was writing at the end of a three-month stay in Corinth on his third missionary journey. On his second journey, he'd spent a year and a half there.

Timothy (verse 21). Timothy was one of Paul's closest associates and chief troubleshooters. He is listed as the co-author of 2 Corinthians, Philippians, Colossians, 1 and 2 Thessalonians, and Philemon, and is, of course, the recipient of 1 and 2 Timothy. Paul sent him to Corinth when that church was divided (1 Corinthians 4:17), and in Philippians 2:19–22, he extolled Timothy's faithfulness.

Lucius (verse 21). This is another form of the name *Luke.* We don't know whether this is Luke, the author of the Gospel and of Acts. But in writing the section of Acts that tells of Paul's journey from Corinth to Jerusalem (Acts 20; 21), Luke used the first-person term *we,* suggesting that he may have been with Paul at the time.

Jason (verse 21). Acts 17:5–9 tells the story of a Jason in Thessalonica who welcomed Paul into his house and was persecuted as a result. But there's no way of knowing whether this is the same Jason.

Tertius (verse 22). This name meant "third." It was almost always slaves who were given names like First, Second, Third, and Fourth. This slave was the scribe who actually wrote down this letter as Paul dictated it to him. This is the only one of Paul's letters for which we know the scribe's name.

Gaius (verse 23). Acts 20:4 says that a Gaius accompanied Paul when he set out for Jerusalem, and in 1 Corinthians 1:14, we find that Paul baptized Gaius at Corinth.

Erastus (verse 23). Paul sends greetings from a man of some prominence—he was the city of Corinth's director of public works. Archaeologists have discovered in Corinth an inscription from the middle of the first century mentioning an Erastus who was the director of streets and who secured his position by constructing a street at his own expense. This almost certainly refers to the same person whose greetings Paul sent to Rome.[3]

Quartus (verse 23). This is the last name Paul mentions. His name means "Fourth," indicating that he, too, was a slave.

Isn't it interesting that the last two names mentioned are those of a slave and a wealthy city official? In other words, the gospel reached a whole spectrum of people from various social classes. The names in this chapter—both those who are greeted in Rome and those who send greetings to Rome—also show that the gospel reached a spectrum of nationalities, for there are Jewish, Greek, and Latin names in these lists.

So, the lists of names in Romans aren't just boring lists of names like those in a telephone book. They're the names of people who are the fruition of the gospel. Those people are the flesh and bones of faith.

For the past seven and a half years, I've had the privilege of serving as a pastor. Currently our membership list has 2,010 names. When I look over this list, it is anything but boring. I see the names of people I've baptized, people I've laughed with, people I've cried with, people I've visited in the hospital, people whose babies I've dedicated, people whose weddings I've had the privilege of performing, people whose spouses I've buried, and so forth. I wish I could say I know all 2,010, but I don't. However, as I look through the names, lots of stories come to mind. I can tell you exactly where many of the people whose names I see sit on Sabbath morning. I see their faces as they sing praises to God. Words cannot begin to describe what these people mean to me.

How appropriate that Paul concludes the book of Romans with these lists of names. The church: believers united together in praise and faith and mission. That is where the book of Romans draws to a close—as it should. Just lists of names—but names that God knows and writes in the book of life.

The final benediction

Paul's final benediction speaks of the *obedience of faith,* a term he used way back in Romans 1:5, where he spoke of Jesus "through whom we have received grace and apostleship to bring about the obedience of faith among all the Gentiles for the sake of his name" (NRSV). Writers in Paul's day often showed what was important by bracketing their work with the same words at the beginning and the end. See if you can figure out what Paul considered most important by comparing the words of Romans 1:5 with his final benediction in Romans 16:25–27.

Now to God who is able to strengthen you according to my gospel and the proclamation of Jesus Christ, according to the revelation of the mystery that was kept secret for long ages but is now disclosed, and through the prophetic writings is made known to all the Gentiles, according to the command of the eternal God, to bring about the obedience of faith—to the only wise God, through Jesus Christ, to whom be the glory forever! Amen (NRSV).

---

1. See Horace, *Sermones,* 1.9.60–78.
2. Paul's spelling of *Priscilla.*
3. For a picture of the inscription, see "Erastus" in the *Seventh-day Adventist Bible Dictionary.*